THE
CHARTER
OF LIBERTY

THE CHARTER OF LIBERTY

The Inspired Origin
and Prophetic Destiny
of the Constitution

William O. Nelson

Deseret Book Company
Salt Lake City, Utah

First printing February 1987

Library of Congress Cataloging-in-Publication Data

Nelson, William O., 1934–
    The charter of liberty.

    Includes index.
        1. Church and state—Mormon Church.   2. United States—
Constitutional law.   3. Mormon Church—Doctrines.
4. Church of Jesus Christ of Latter-day Saints—
Doctrines.   I. Title.
BX8643.P6N45 1987   261.7   86-32821
ISBN 0-87579-075-5

May those principles, which were so
honorably and nobly defended, namely,
the Constitution of our land, by our
fathers, be established forever.

Doctrine and Covenants 109:54

Contents

"We Will Stand by Its Principles"

No greater immediate responsibility rests upon members of the Church, upon all citizens of this Republic and of neighboring Republics, than to protect the freedom vouchsafed by the Constitution of the United States.

President David O. McKay

Latter-day Saint doctrine clearly supports the view of an inspired constitution. By inspired, we mean that God miraculously impressed on the minds of the Founding Fathers the "just and holy principles" contained in the Constitution that would preserve the basic rights of the people. Also inspired were their efforts in producing a final document that represented the will of the majority of the Convention of 1787.[1] A compelling motivation of Latter-day Saints to support the Constitution is the Lord's admonition by revelation to befriend "that law which is the constitutional law of the land." (D&C 98:6.) Moreover, the Prophet Joseph Smith is reported to have said that the Constitution would one day hang by a thread and that if it were to be saved, it would be saved by members of the Church.[2]

The statement by Joseph Smith is regarded as prophetic and implies an apostasy from the original principles that were laid down to preserve basic freedoms. That apostasy from the principles is well documented. President John Taylor said in 1884, "By and by, you will find they will tear the Constitution to shreds, as they have begun now; they won't have to begin; they have started long ago to rend the

1

Constitution of our country in pieces; and in doing so they are letting loose and encouraging a principle which will react upon themselves with terrible consequences."[3] President J. Reuben Clark, Jr., gave a number of discourses on the subject that are preserved in his writings.[4] He deplored administrative agencies being empowered to make laws; the office of the president of the United States assuming war powers during so-called emergencies; the breaking down of the independence of the three branches of government— executive, judicial, and legislative; the diminishing of local self-government and the increasing centralization of the federal government; the powers used by the federal government to redistribute the wealth of its citizens from one sector of the economy to another; of immigrants who brought with them an alien philosophy into the country, some of whom served in bureaucratic agencies of government; and the diminishing of the protections to the people's Bill of Rights—all these, he noted, were departures and usurpations of the provisions to the Constitution that should not be warranted by the people. Other respected legal scholars have also noted the departure from the original principles of the Constitution.[5]

How Will the Constitution Be Saved?

How members of the Church should step forward to save the Constitution from the verge of destruction is subject to interpretation. A popular view is that they should seek political office, and, by virtue of their political influence, defend constitutional principles. Another view is that members of the Church must learn constitutional principles and then insist that their elected representatives adhere to those principles. While there is some merit to both these perspectives, still another interpretation was given by President John Taylor. Said he:

> We have got to establish a government upon the principle of righteousness, justice, truth and equality and not according to the many false notions that exist among men. And then the day is not far distant when this nation will be

shaken from the centre to circumference. . . . When the people shall have torn to shreds the Constitution of the United States *the Elders of Israel will be found holding it up to the nations of the earth and proclaiming liberty and equal rights to all men, and extending the hand of fellowship to the oppressed of all nations.* This is part of the programme, and as long as we do what is right and fear God, he will help us and stand by us under all circumstances.[6]

The implication of this interpretation is that the Saints, because of their faith and testimony of the Constitution, will never abandon its fundamental principles even though the nation as a whole may apostatize from them. In light of prophecies from the Book of Mormon and the Prophet Joseph Smith, such a departure from true principles is not unlikely.[7]

Another implication of John Taylor's prophecy is that members of the Church will defend and uphold the underlying principles of the Constitution regardless of where they live. This does not mean that Church members will be insubordinate to the laws or the political structure of the governments of their respective countries, but it implies that they, in conscience, will give allegiance to those principles that accord to man his fundamental rights.

The Constitution for "All Flesh"

John Taylor's declaration that the elders of the Church will uphold its principles to the nations of the earth is consistent with the Lord's revelation that the Constitution of the United States was to be maintained for the rights and protection of "all flesh." (See D&C 101:77.) What is meant by "all flesh?" Does the prophecy mean that the Constitution's provisions are intended for all people?

That the principles of the Constitution are intended for all people, regardless of nationality, is evident from the aforementioned revelation. Unless the agency of all people is respected and freedom is accorded to all, they cannot be fully accountable for their own sins. Moreover, since it is "not right that any man should be in bondage one to another" (D&C 101:79), the principles of the Constitution have validity for all people in all nations.[8]

Does the Constitution for "all flesh" mean that other governments should or will adopt principles from the U. S. Constitution? President J. Reuben Clark, Jr., expressed in a general priesthood conference that some nations had already adopted the "great essentials" from the Constitution:

> I will recall . . . to your attention, that the Constitution of the United States is the basic law for all of the Americas, or Zion, as it has been defined by the Lord.
>
> You brethren from Canada know that your great British North America Act, in its fundamental principles, is based upon our Constitution, and you know that in the courts of Canada, the reports of our Supreme Court, and our Federal courts generally, are just as persuasive as the decisions of the courts of England, and even more so, where questions of constitutional law and constitutional interpretation are involved.
>
> You brethren also know that from the Rio Grande down to the Horn there is no constitutional government except those that are founded primarily upon our own Constitution. In Mexico the revolutionary party which more than a century and a quarter ago rebelled against the king of Spain and established a republic, copied almost verbatim, and practically overnight, our Constitution, and made it their own. Neither Mexico nor the others to the South interpret their Constitutions as we interpret ours. They have different standards and different canons of interpretation, for their fundamental system is the civil law, while ours is the common law. But the great essentials of that document, the Constitution of the United States, which God Himself inspired, is the law of Zion, the Americas.[9]

But there is another significant meaning to the prophecy that the elders of Israel will uphold the principles of the Constitution to the nations of the earth. In recent years, Latter-day Saints have been urged to reflect on the meaning of the Constitution and to live by its principles.[10] A burden is therefore placed on the Saints to learn the fundamental principles of the Constitution and then to uphold them. An example would be that Church members believe that all people have the right to worship God according to their own conscience. (Article of Faith 11.) Should Church members do other than support the principles of the Constitution that assure the expression of this right?

Indeed, those who become members of The Church of Jesus Christ of Latter-day Saints give tacit approval to the underlying principles of the Constitution by virtue of sustaining latter-day revelation.[11]

The Constitution is a prosaic document, and its words, phrases, and clauses have been subject to many decisions of the courts. The tendency of many people, therefore, is to neglect the meaning of the document. President John Taylor's prophecy further implies that Church members need not necessarily be experts in the technicalities of constitutional law, but they must be familiar with its fundamental principles so they can uphold them. Such a view is consistent with the testimony of Elder Harold B. Lee: "Would it be sacrilegious to paraphrase the words of the Apostle Peter, and say that the Constitution of the United States could be saved by the elders of this Church because this Church and this Church alone has the words of eternal life? We alone know by revelation as to how the Constitution came into being, and we, alone, know by revelation the destiny of this nation. The preservation of 'life, liberty and the pursuit of happiness' can be guaranteed upon no other basis than upon a sincere faith and testimony of the divinity of these teachings."[12]

When members of the Church uphold the principles that underlie the Constitution and proclaim liberty and equal rights, the Constitution will indeed be for "all flesh" in all nations.

The Story of Our Constitution

The succeeding chapters of this book tell the story of the remarkable spiritual achievement of the framers of the Constitution in securing an unparalleled freedom for the citizens of the United States. Their accomplishment is placed within a religious, not just a political context. In this sense, it is an untold saga. Told from a Latter-day Saint theological perspective, the story relates how a distinguished assembly of statesmen, by virtue of premortal assignment, came together at one place at a singular time in history to accomplish a monumental feat. They devised a government in which freedom of religion was secured. From such a climate of liberty, the gospel was restored and then extended from the shores of America to other nations. Thus we see the beginning of the fulfillment of the ancient prophecy that "out of Zion shall go forth the law." (Isaiah 2:3.)

The Constitution was constructed by tough, arduous labor—by imperfect men who were instruments in God's hands in achieving His divine purpose. Their willingness to compromise for the good of a union made possible a "land of liberty" as prophesied in the Book of Mormon.

Paradoxically, for the Saints, the land of liberty that guaranteed religious freedom became a land of religious persecution for over seven decades into the twentieth century. In the context of that persecution, the Lord gave His approbation to the Constitution and its principles and counseled the Saints to exercise restraint and seek legal redress, not retaliation. Their forbearance made it possible that those who interfered with their rights and deprived them of their liberties would be held accountable before God in the day of His judgment.

As the Book of Mormon shows, virtue is absolutely necessary for this nation to survive. Freedom today, fragile as it is, depends on total virtue. The electorate must be virtuous. If the citizens of this nation do not practice virtue and live by the restraints placed on them by their Creator; if they become intemperate in their wants and yield to politicians who pander to their pleadings, they will lose their freedom. But there must also be virtue among those elected to public trust by the people. If the elected become morally derelict, it is incumbent on the electorate to remove them. Only virtue in both the elected and the electorate will preserve our freedoms. When virtue is ignored or neglected, the Constitution indeed "hangs by a thread," and the nation becomes subject to the same divine decree that brought other nations that have occupied this land to destruction. (See Ether 2:9-12.)

Are We an Idolatrous People?

Are we at that point today? We are perilously close. During the nation's Bicentennial, a prophet of the Lord—President Spencer W. Kimball—equated our sins with the idolatry practiced by the Israelites in ancient times:

> The Brethren constantly cry out against that which is intolerable in the sight of the Lord: against pollution of mind, body, and our surroundings; against vulgarity, stealing, lying, pride, and blasphemy; against fornication, adultery, homosexuality, and all other abuses of the sacred power to create; against murder and all that is like unto it; against all manner of desecration.
>
> That such a cry should be necessary among a people so blessed is amazing to me. And that such things should be found even among the Saints to some degree is scarcely believable, for these are a people who are in possession of many gifts of the Spirit, who have knowledge that puts the eternities into perspective, who have been shown the way to eternal life.
>
> Sadly, however, we find that to be shown the way is not necessarily to walk in it, and many have not been able to continue in faith. These have submitted themselves in one degree or another to the enticings of Satan and his servants and joined with those of "the world" in lies of ever-deepening idolatry.
>
> I use the word *idolatry* intentionally. As I study ancient scripture, I am more and more convinced that there is significance in the fact that the commandment "Thou shalt have no other gods before me" is the first of the Ten Commandments.
>
> Few men have ever knowingly and deliberately chosen to reject God and his blessings. Rather, we learn from the scriptures that because the exercise of faith has always appeared to be more difficult than relying on things more immediately at hand, carnal man has tended

to transfer his trust in God to material things. Therefore, in all ages when men have fallen under the power of Satan and lost the faith, they have put in its place a hope in the "arm of flesh" and in "gods of silver, and gold, of brass, iron, wood, and stone, which see not, nor hear, nor know" (Daniel 5:23)—that is, in idols. This I find to be a dominant theme in the Old Testament. Whatever thing a man sets his heart and his trust in most is his god; and if his god doesn't also happen to be the true and living God of Israel, that man is laboring in idolatry.

It is my firm belief that when we read these scriptures and try to "liken them unto [our]selves," as Nephi suggested (1 Nephi 19:24), *we will see many parallels between the ancient worship of graven images and behavioral patterns in our very experience.*

The Lord has blessed us as a people with a prosperity unequaled in times past. The resources that have been placed in our power are good, and necessary to our work here on the earth. But I am afraid that many of us have been surfeited with flocks and herds and acres and barns and wealth and have begun to worship them as false gods, and they have power over us. Do we have more of these good things than our faith can stand? Many people spend most of their time working in the service of a self-image that includes sufficient money, stocks, bonds, investment portfolios, property, credit cards, furnishings, automobiles, and the like to *guarantee* carnal security throughout, it is hoped, a long and happy life. Forgotten is the fact that our assignment is to use these many resources in our families and quorums to build up the kingdom of God—to further the missionary effort and the genealogical and temple work; to raise our children up as fruitful servants unto the Lord; to bless others in every way, that they may also be fruitful. Instead, we expend these blessings on our own desires, and as Moroni said, "Ye adorn yourselves with that which hath no life, and yet suffer the hungry, and the needy, and the naked, and the sick and the afflicted to pass by you, and notice them not." (Mormon 8:39.)

As the Lord himself said in our day, "They seek not the Lord to establish his righteousness, but every man

walketh in his own way, and after the image of his own
God, whose image is in the likeness of the world, and
whose substance is that of an idol, which waxeth old and
shall perish in Babylon, even Babylon the great, which
shall fall." (D&C 1:16; italics added.)[13]

Such an indictment—especially as it was directed to
members of the Church—should give us pause and the
desire to repent and turn our hearts to a gracious Heavenly
Father who has bestowed on us such bounteous gifts—one
of the most precious of which is our freedom.

We Will Stand by Its Principles

Our freedom depends not so much on what we know
about the Constitution, but on whether we understand its
fundamental principles and then live righteous, virtuous
lives. When we do that, we will influence others by "proclaiming liberty and equal rights to all men, and extending
the hand of fellowship to the oppressed of all nations." We
shall then be prepared to fulfill another of President John
Taylor's prophecies even though others may apostatize
from the principles that have secured our rights: "If law-
makers and administrators can afford to trample upon
justice, equity, and the Constitution of this country, they
will find thousands and tens of thousands who are willing to
follow in their wake in the demolition of the rights of man,
and the destruction of all principles of justice, and the
safeguards of the nation but *we will stand by and maintain
its principles and the rights of all men of every color, and
every clime; we will cleave to the truth, live our religion and
keep the commandments of God, and God will bless us in
time and throughout the eternities that are to come."*[14]

And again he prophesied, "It may not be among the
improbabilities, that the prophecies of Joseph Smith may be
fulfilled and that the calumniated and despised Mormons
may yet become the protectors of the Constitution and the
guardians of religious liberty and human freedom in these
United States."[15]

"The Best Spirits God Could Find"

The Framers of our Constitution knew . . . history. . . . They were trained and experienced in the Common Law. They remembered the Barons and King John at Runnymede. They were thoroughly indoctrinated in the principle that the true sovereignty rested in the people.

J. Reuben Clark, Jr.

An extraordinary occurrence took place in St. George, Utah, just over one hundred years after the Declaration of Independence was signed. The St. George Temple had been dedicated in April 1877 amid great rejoicing and prayers of thanksgiving. It was now August, and Wilford Woodruff, the new president of the St. George Temple, was at the temple during the late night hours. Several weeks later, he disclosed what had transpired on that night, the next two days, and the following night. "The spirits of the dead gathered around me," he said, "wanting to know why we did not redeem them."[1] He identified them as the signers of the Declaration of Independence and other eminent leaders who came to him "for two days and two nights." The majority of the thirty-nine signers of the Constitution had received proxy baptism and confirmations in the Endowment House almost one year before.[2] But the proxy ordinance work for the signers of the Declaration of Independence had not been done. They were dismayed that their ordinances had not been done, because they had laid the foundation for a new government. Recalling their appearance in later years, Wilford Woodruff said that these spirits *demanded* at his hands that he "should go forth and attend to the ordinances of the House of God for them."[3] They said to President Woodruff: "You have had use of the Endowment House for a number of years, and yet nothing has been done for us. We laid the foundation of the government you now enjoy, and we never apostatized from it, but we remained true to it and were faithful to God."[4]

Accordingly, on August 21, 1877, Elder Wilford Woodruff and Brother R. D. McAllister performed the proxy ordinances for these and other eminent persons in the St. George Temple. Elder Woodruff recorded in his journal:

> When Br McAllister had Baptized me for the 100 Names I Baptized him for 21, including Gen Washington & his forefathers and all the Presidents of the United States that were not in my list Except Buchannan Van Buren & Grant.
>
> It was a vary interesting day. I felt thankful that we had the privilege and the power to administer for the worthy dead esspecially for the signers of the declaration of Independence, that inasmuch as they had laid the foundation of our Government that we could do as much for them as they had done for us.
>
> Sister Lucy Bigelow Young went forth into the font and was Baptized for Martha Washington and her famaly and seventy (70) of the Eminent women of the world. I Called upon all the Brethren & Sisters who were present to assist in getting Endowments for those that we had been Baptized for to day.[5]

Church historians have been noticeably quiescent about this remarkable episode. Earlier that year, however, Wilford Woodruff recorded pointedly in his journal: "I warn the future historians to give credence to my history; for my testimony is true, and the truth of its record will be manifest in the world to come."[6]

The testimony of Wilford Woodruff is extraordinary for several reasons. First, it implies that there was a collective virtue among the men responsible for the founding principles of the American nation. They collaborated in mortal-

ity to lay down the principles that established the government of the United States and then mutually appeared to
Wilford Woodruff with the appeal to perform ordinance
work for them. "Would those spirits have called upon me to
perform that work," said Wilford Woodruff, "if they had
not been noble spirits before God?"[7]

Second, the fact that these men who came to Wilford
Woodruff "demanded" ordinances of salvation signifies
their acknowledgement and acceptance of gospel principles
that were restored some forty years after they had established a free government. This demonstrates a connection
between the work they performed and the restoration of the
gospel of Jesus Christ to this dispensation.

Third, Wilford Woodruff's testimony that the founders
said to him that they "laid the foundation of the government
[we] now enjoy" further implies that what they accomplished was the will of God. This testimony corroborates a
revelation given to the Prophet Joseph Smith in 1833 in
which the Lord said that the Constitution of the United
States had been established "by the hands of wise men
whom I raised up *unto this very purpose.*" (D&C 101:80;
italics added.)

An Aggregation of Exceptional Talent

Historians are generally agreed that never before had
there been such an assembly of men gathered to determine
the kind of government to which they would give their allegiance. Thomas Jefferson exclaimed that the framers of the
Constitution were "demigods," and other eminent writers
have concurred with J. Reuben Clark's assessment that there
has never been a "group that . . . challenged the supremacy
of this group."[8]

How does one account for such an assembly of talent at
one time and one place in history? Generally it is treated
as a fortuitous, chance circumstance when an opportune
moment in history brought forth such talent.[9]

A more perceptive, reasonable, and equitable explanation that accounts for such extraordinary talents and abilities

among men was offered by the Prophet Joseph Smith. On
the basis of revelation, he declared the unique truth that all
men and women lived before their mortal birth and that
exceptional abilities were the result of faithfulness and effort
in one's premortal life. Such an explanation is reasonable
and just because it postulates that all people had something
to do with developing their talents and abilities before they
were born, rather than that God discriminately favored a
few of His children with talents while depriving others of
the same.

The doctrine of man's premortality provides us with
some expansive insights. Based on the Christian principle of
the Fatherhood of God, fundamentally the doctrine is: all
mortal beings are the spirit offspring of God and premortally
dwelt in His presence as His spirit children. Because each received his or her spirit existence from Him, God is the literal
Father of all mankind.

In premortal life, spirits had agency and progressed in
knowledge and intelligence in proportion to the obedience
that they gave to the eternal laws of God. Not all spirits
made the same effort or gave the same degree of obedience
to eternal law. Accordingly, spirits developed different
talents and aptitudes—intellectual, musical, artistic, and
spiritual.[10] The Lord revealed to Abraham this principle:
"These two facts do exist, that there are two spirits, one
being more intelligent than the other; there shall be another
more intelligent than they; I am the Lord thy God, I am
more intelligent than they all." (Abraham 3:19.) Here we
have at least three degrees of intelligences or spirits: one is
more intelligent than another—a third is more intelligent
than the other two. There were, in other words, gradations
in intelligence. Differences among persons born into mortal-
ity are based on their premortal initiative and obedience,
accounting for individuality and exceptional and extraordinary talents. In Latter-day Saint theology, there never
was, there is not now, nor will there ever be equality of
intelligence.[11]

In the account revealed to Joseph Smith, Abraham was
shown the premortal spirit children of God, whom he de-

scribed as "the intelligences that were organized before the world was." He saw "many of the noble and great ones." Standing among these valiant spirits, God saw that "they were good." Abraham was "one of them" and was "chosen before [he] wast born." (Abraham 3:22-23.)

Prophets of God, considered as the "noble and great," came to earth to accomplish assignments given by God in premortal councils. "Every man," said Joseph Smith, "who has a calling to minister to the inhabitants of the world was ordained to that very purpose in the Grand Council of heaven before the world was."[12] Other male and female spirits, also noble, are given assignments to further the progress of mankind. Significantly, Wilford Woodruff declared the founders of the American Republic to be "the best spirits the God of heaven could find on the face of the earth. They were choice spirits."[13]

The doctrine of our premortal life increases our reverence for God's omniscience. Only an omniscient God could direct the timing and placement of His children on this earth. Only God can providentially determine to what nation His children will be sent. Timing and placement are crucial to the accomplishment of His divine purposes. Thus, the assignment of select sons and daughters to come to earth at particular places and at a particular historical moment is neither haphazard nor accidental. Both Moses and the Apostle Paul implied this truth in their writings,[14] but it took latter-day revelation to clarify our understanding of it.

With the perspective that we had a premortal life, we can see that it was not an accident of history that such an assembly of talent appeared on the scene at one time and in one nation. They came to earth by assignment from God; this assignment, according to their words to Wilford Woodruff, was to "lay a foundation" of a new government that would provide freedom to all. That freedom was a necessary precursor for a later restoration of the gospel. That is why the founders of the American republic are rightfully respected in Church theology as necessary forerunners to the great latter-day work of establishing the kingdom of God on earth before the Savior comes again.

Intellectual and Spiritual Influences on the Founders

Historians have not been oblivious to the intellectual and religious influences that gave rise to the unique American political system embodied in the Declaration of Independence and the Constitution. The fundamental doctrine of government through the rule of law rather than government through the rule of a sovereign was not a unique idea of the Founding Fathers. Previous political thinkers had enunciated this idea centuries before, but their ideas were not fully developed until the framers of the Constitution collaborated to debate the kind of government under which they would live. Happily, the framers were familiar with history, common law, and philosophy. They may have traveled in horse-drawn carriages, but they "carried under their hats . . . a political wisdom garnered from the ages."[15]

That political wisdom included belief in four fundamental principles: First, a belief in the natural rights of man; second, that people cannot be taxed without their consent; third, that the best way to preserve liberty is to separate and limit the powers of government; and fourth, that the powers of self-government could be delegated to representatives of their own choosing.

As British subjects, the framers brought to the Constitutional Convention the British common law precedent of rights and liberties. These rights and liberties had been secured by centuries of struggle wherein the Britons won concessions from kings who held to the Justinian Code that "the prince stood above the law."[16] That view represented the European continental conception of government, that he who rules holds all power, rights, and authority.

The first political concession that limited a monarch's power was made on June 12, 1215, when King John was compelled to sign the Magna Charta. The Great Charter established two principles that form the basis for English constitutional law. First, there are certain laws that even the king is compelled to obey; and second, if the monarch (government) refuses to obey these laws, the nation has the legitimate right to overthrow the government. This historic right was later invoked by the colonists in the Declaration of Independence when they stated that the king of England had so infringed upon the rights of his subjects that he was "no longer fitted to be the ruler of a free people."

In the seventeenth century, Parliament presented to Charles I a Petition of Rights. The petition was a reassertion of the provisions of the Magna Charta, demanding that the king agree to what was already the law of the land. The king was unwilling to acknowledge these provisions, so Parliament demanded his formal consent. Charles I resisted. But because he needed money to operate his government, and because Parliament refused to vote him money until he agreed to their petition, he reluctantly signed the petition on June 7, 1628. He thereafter dissolved Parliament and refused to grant the rights to which he had agreed. For that, he was subsequently carried to the scaffold and beheaded.

The monarchy was not restored until 1660, when Charles II agreed to the provisions of the Magna Charta and the Petition of Rights. However, his brother, James II, who succeeded him, reasserted the right of absolute monarchy. In the Revolution of 1688, James was forced to abdicate, and parliamentary rule was established once and for all among the British people.

In 1689, Parliament established a constitutional landmark—the Bill of Rights. The Bill of Rights provided in written form specific rights of the people that are fundamental to British constitutional law. Excessive bail, fines, and cruel and unusual punishment were declared illegal. Only Parliament could levy taxes. The bill also gave citizens the rights to bear arms. The king could not suspend laws or create courts outside of established law.

England's revolution was between the monarch and Parliament. Out of this struggle emerged the by-product— liberty for British citizens. So profound was the impact of the revolution upon the Puritan settlers in America that they instituted the same principles in their colonial government —principles that had been won by centuries of struggle. That struggle, however, established in the minds of the British subjects the idea of government by law rather than

government by a sovereign. A century later this would find
expression in the Constitution and the first eight amendments to the Constitution.

John Locke's ideas formed the basis for both the English
and the American revolutions. His *Two Treatises of Government* was not published until two years after the English
Revolution, but the manuscript had been in existence for
twenty years, so his ideas were well known. According to
Locke, all people have certain natural rights, which consist
of life, liberty, and property. In order to protect these rights,
people form a government by social contract. Government,
he reasoned, has certain powers to govern so long as it rules
fairly and equitably in preserving the rights of the people.
Should government break the contract by arbitrarily removing these unalienable rights, those governed are relieved
of their contract. They then had the absolute right to rebel
and to establish a new government.

Other key ideas of Locke—sovereignty of the people,
government resting on the consent of the governed; the
legislature as the supreme power but its power delegated by
the people, who may withdraw it; and the executive as the
agent of the legislature—provided the fundamental philosophy for the colonists.

Another idea that found expression in the American
system was the belief that liberty could be preserved by
limiting government. Baron de Montesquieu conceived that
the best way to achieve this was by separating the powers of
government into three departments: executive, legislative,
and judicial. The doctrine of separation of powers is a cardi-
nal feature of the U. S. Constitution.

There were also undeniable Christian influences on the
founders that sponsored their ideas about civil liberties as
expressed in the Bill of Rights. Moreover, the entire American legal tradition (judicial review of government acts, presumption of innocence of the accused, compensation to
those negligently injured, equal protection of the right of a
person to have a court determine reason for his or her de-
tention) is based on biblical justification.[17]

But a written constitution was not conceived only from

the ideas of these preceding philosophers and events. For 169 years, the colonists experimented with varying forms of government under British rule. In some instances, they had substantial autonomy of rule. Through experience with charters, colonial legislatures, and later state constitutions, they learned the value of self-government as a means to secure their liberty.[18] But even though some local autonomy had been granted to the colonists, Parliament still insisted on regulating colonial commerce through navigation acts and through levying taxes.

Precipitating Causes of the American Revolution

Resistance to taxation by the colonists rested on the historical British constitution that it was unlawful to tax without the consent of citizens through lawfully appointed representatives. The colonists, of course, had no representation in Parliament, so they denied that Parliament had the right to tax them. When the British imposed the dreaded Stamp Act and enforced it by the innovation of admiralty courts, the colonists reacted violently. The most notable firebrand of the revolution, Patrick Henry, denounced the act as illegal. The act was subsequently repealed, but the British government insisted on the supremacy of Parliament to maintain its right to tax and to regulate commerce. This disagreement reached a crisis with the Boston Tea Party and resistance to other acts regarded by the colonists as unlawful. They took their first steps toward union by sending representatives to the First Continental Congress in 1774. The delegates made a list of grievances and asserted their right to live as British subjects. Britain refused to redress their grievances. Hostilities then broke out in Massachusetts when local farmers attacked British troops at Lexington and Concord. The British declared Massachusetts in a state of rebellion.

When the Second Continental Congress convened in May 1775, some members of Congress still hoped for reconciliation. Again Congress petitioned England. King George dismissed their petition with contempt and pronounced them rebels. Finding that they could not have the rights of

English citizens, the colonists rebelled, and the revolution commenced.

Momentous events in history are the result of colliding influences: the personalities in a drama, an issue or a crisis, and a timing that synchronizes these influences into a historically significant event.

We can hardly imagine a greater confluence of forces— an issue that had crescendoed for centuries, a king who desired to preserve the view that he who has power has the right to dictate, and the colonists who were willing to sacrifice their lives to be independent from oppression. Had it not been for the collision of these opposing philosophies and personalities the American Revolution might never have occurred. Brigham Young intimated as much when he said: "The king of Great Britain . . . might . . . have been led to . . . aggressive acts, for aught we know, to bring to pass the purposes of God in thus establishing a new government upon a principle of greater freedom, a basis of self-government allowing the free exercise of religious worship."[19]

The Revolution Was Foreordained

That the American Revolution was foreknown by God and foreordained to happen is evident from some remarkable prophecies from the Book of Mormon, which were recorded some twenty-three hundred years before the revolution transpired.

Prophecy	*Commentary*
I looked and beheld a man among the Gentiles, who was separated from the seed of my brethren by the many waters; and I beheld the Spirit of God, that it came down and wrought upon the man; and he went	The "man among the Gentiles" has been interpreted as being Christopher Columbus.

forth upon the many waters, even unto the seed of my brethren, who were in the promised land. (1 Nephi 13:12.)

I beheld the Spirit of God, that it wrought upon other Gentiles; and they went forth out of captivity, upon the many waters.

And it came to pass that I beheld many multitudes of the Gentiles upon the land of promise; and I beheld the wrath of God, that it was upon the seed of my brethren; and they were scattered before the Gentiles and were smitten. (1 Nephi 13:13-14.)

The "other Gentiles" that came out of captivity were the Puritans, Pilgrims, and others who sought freedom. The "seed of my brethren" were Nephi's brethren, namely Lamanites or their descendants, the Indian of the Western hemisphere. Their scattering and decimation by the explorers and later the colonists is an established fact.

And I beheld the Spirit of the Lord, that it was upon the Gentiles, and they did prosper and obtain the land for their inheritance. (1 Nephi 13:15.)

The Gentiles are essentially our European ancestors who migrated to America.

I, Nephi, beheld that the Gentiles who had gone forth out of captivity did humble themselves before the Lord; and the power of the Lord was with them. (1 Nephi 13:16.)

And I beheld that their mother Gentiles were gathered together upon the waters, and upon the land also, to battle against them.

And I beheld that the power of God was with them, and also that the wrath of God was upon

The "mother Gentiles" is the mother country—Great Britain.

all those that were gathered together against them to battle.

And I, Nephi, beheld that the Gentiles that had gone out of captivity were delivered by the power of God out of the hands of all other nations. (1 Nephi 13:17-19.)

The power of God, not the military genius of George Washington, delivered the colonists out of the hands of the mother country, Great Britain.

What is so remarkable about the outcome of the Revolutionary War is that the Colonists should not have won. The British were better equipped, had a better trained army, and had more experienced leadership. How a ragtag revolutionary army won against superior forces is, in some measure, attributable to the leadership of General Washington; but, as the eminent Winston Churchill wrote, there was a more significant factor:

> Rarely has British strategy fallen into such a multitude of errors. Every maxim and principle of war was either violated or disregarded "Seek out and destroy the enemy" is a sound rule. "Concentrate your force" is a sound method. "Maintain your objective" is common sense. The enemy was Washington's army. The force consisted of Howe's troops in New York and Burgoyne's columns now assembled in Montreal. The objective was to destroy Washington's army and kill or capture Washington. If he could be brought to battle, and every man and gun turned against him, a British victory was almost certain. But *these obvious truths were befogged and bedevilled by multiplicity of counsel.*[20]

Churchill explained from a secular perspective what the Prophet Nephi had prophesied six hundred years before Christ—that the wrath of God was on those who opposed the colonists, and the power of God delivered them. (See 1 Nephi 13:19.)

On July 2, 1776, the Continental Congress approved the Declaration of Independence. Borrowing from English heritage, the declaration forcefully asserted that "all men are created equal"; "that they are endowed by their Creator with certain unalienable rights"; "that among these are life, liberty, and the pursuit of happiness"; "that to secure these rights, governments are instituted among men, deriving their just powers from the consent of the governed"; "that whenever any form of government becomes destructive of these ends, it is the right of the people to alter or to abolish it, and to institute new government, laying its foundation on such principles, and organizing its powers in such form, as to them shall seem most likely to effect their safety and happiness." The declaration noted: "When a long train of abuses and usurpations, pursuing invariably the same object, evinces a design to reduce them under absolute despotism, it is their right, it is their duty, to throw off such government, and to provide new guards for their future security." (See appendix 2.)

In approving the declaration, the colonists based their revolution on an appeal to a higher law than man—the natural rights doctrine that "all men are created equal" and that God had given all people unalienable rights of life, liberty, and property. If they could not enjoy their rights as British subjects, they would become independent of Britain. If they could not be equal with the English *in* the British Empire, they would be equal to the English *outside* the Empire, but as members of the human race.

The declaration was a climax of humanity's centuries-long struggle for rights and liberty.

Conclusion

The galaxy of incomparable leaders that came on the scene at one time and in one place to provide the world with an ensign of liberty was divinely directed. God held these men in reserve to come forth at a precise moment in history to declare independence for a nation that was foreordained to be a sanctuary of freedom. They were not insurrectionists. Their revolution was an appeal to higher law that entitled them to revolt against any government that broke its contract to preserve their unalienable rights. It was done in recognition of natural rights and the established precedent of British common law. Once the revolution was accomplished, these leaders demonstrated their virtue by establishing a new government that ensured to all citizens their God-given rights.

2

"We Laid the Foundation"

I established the Constitution of this land, by the
hands of wise men *whom I raised up* unto this
very purpose. (D&C 101:80; italics added.)

A natural curiosity exists about those who laid
the foundation of the American republic. Who
were they? What was their background? Why
did the Lord designate them as men of
wisdom?

Most of the fifty-five delegates to the Constitutional Convention were in the prime of life, their average age being forty-two. Four were in their twenties, twenty-one were younger than forty, and fourteen were over fifty. They were generally men of exceptional character, well-educated, politically experienced, and distinguished in their professions. For the most part, they were religious men. Significantly, none were atheists.

Twenty-nine of the fifty-five were educated in the leading American colleges and in Great Britain. There were nine Princeton graduates, three from Harvard, and four from Yale. Thirty-four had legal training; fourteen were or had been lawyers or judges; six had been or were to be state attorney generals; and five had been or would later be chief justices of state supreme courts.

Forty-two had seen service in the Continental Congress. Seven had signed the Declaration of Independence. Six had signed the Articles of Confederation. Thirty of the forty-three living signers supported the Constitution. Forty-six had served in state legislatures, ten had attended state constitutional conventions, and sixteen had been or would later serve as governors.

25

At least thirty had served in the revolutionary army, eighteen as officers; four had been on Washington's personal staff during the war.

Among that assembly of the fifty-five delegates were two future presidents of the United States; a vice-president; a secretary of the treasury; a secretary of war; a secretary of state; two chief justices of the Supreme Court, and three who served as justices. Fourteen were to be congressmen; nineteen would become senators; and four were to be cabinet members. And there was the venerable Franklin— diplomat, philosopher, scientist, and statesman.

Let us now look briefly at the thirty-nine delegates who were signatories to the Constitution. Their names appear in the order they signed the document, and the bracketed number is their age at the time of their signing.

President of the Convention

The most illustrious of the signers was *George Washington* (55). As a youth, he was tutored by his half-brother, Lawrence, whom he idolized. At age fifteen, he left school and became a surveyor. At twenty, he was commissioned a major in the Virginia militia and was subsequently promoted to colonel. By age twenty-three, he was appointed commander in chief of the Virginia militia. Through marriage to a wealthy widow, and through his own inheritance, Washington became one of the wealthiest men in the colonies.

He was later elected as a Virginia delegate to the first and second Continental congresses. When asked who was the greatest man in Congress, Patrick Henry said, "If you speak of solid information and sound judgment, Colonel Washington is unquestionably the greatest man on that floor." Washington supported Henry's resolution for independence from Britain in 1775.

At great personal sacrifice, Washington came out of retirement and left his family, his friends, and his beloved Mt. Vernon to accept the commission as commander in chief of the Continental army. Overcoming incredible odds, he defeated the British army and became the hero of the revolution. When he retired his commission, he said: "I consider it an indispensable duty to close this last act of my official life by commending the interests of our dearest country to the protection of Almighty God, and those who have the superintendence of them to his holy keeping."

When it became apparent that the peace that was won during the revolution would not last under the Articles of Confederation, Washington acceded to his election by the Virginia legislature to the Constitutional Convention.

His greatest contribution at the convention was in acting as the presiding officer. During the ninety-nine days of the convention's proceedings in the heat of summer, Washington calmly guided the sometimes turbulent sessions. Unquestionably, his approval of the new Constitution was its greatest single endorsement. After ratification of the Constitution, Washington was the only logical candidate for president.

At his inauguration as the nation's first president, Washington took the oath of office to defend the Constitution of the United States. He then bowed his head, kissed the Bible, and with reverent feeling uttered, "So help me God!"[1]

With the Old World watching carefully what they considered as the new American experiment, Washington provided a remarkable example of statesmanship. As a soldier, he had literally beat his sword into a plowshare; he had refused the efforts of his soldiers to make him a king; and after serving eight years as the first president of the United States, he stepped down and let his successor be elected by the procedures set forth in the new Constitution.

In his famous farewell address, Washington warned against geographical discriminations, party strife, hatred toward other nations, and foreign entanglements, but he also cautioned that a nation could not maintain its moral virtue without the indispensable support of religion: "Let us with caution indulge the supposition, that morality can be maintained without religion. Whatever may be conceded to the influence of refined education on minds of peculiar structure, reason and experience both forbid us to expect that National morality can prevail in exclusion of religious principle."[2]

Thomas Jefferson said of him, "His integrity was most pure, his justice the most inflexible I have ever known, no motives or consanguinity of friendship or hatred being able to bias his decision. He was indeed, . . . a wise, a good and great man. . . . On the whole, his character was . . . perfect, in nothing bad."[3]

New Hampshire

John Langdon (46) was a wealthy shipowner who helped finance the revolution by building the first American warship, the *Ranger*. Through his influence and money, he raised New Hampshire troops for the war, served as an officer, and made possible the victory at Bennington in 1777. He served as a delegate to the Continental Congress. He paid the expenses for himself and fellow delegate Nicolas Gilman to the Philadelphia Convention. He represented the small states in the debates and single-handedly persuaded other delegates in New Hampshire to ratify the Constitution. As a result, New Hampshire became the ninth state to ratify, which provided a majority to establish the new government. After the Constitution's ratification, he served for twelve years in the United States Senate, being the first temporary president (pro tempore). On April 6, 1789, he personally counted the first electoral votes and informed Washington of his election as first president of the United States.

Of Langdon's character, Madison wrote: "He was a true patriot and a good man with a noble way of thinking and a frankness and warmth of heart that made his friends love him much, as it did me."[4]

Nicholas Gilman (32) a bachelor, served as an officer in the Revolutionary War. He was nicknamed "Congress" Gilman because of his cocky attitude and his ambition to make politics a career. He arrived late to the convention and, according to the record, made little contribution to the proceedings. Gilman served for seventeen years in Congress as a representative and a senator.

Massachusetts

Nathaniel Gorham (49) had served as president of the Continental Congress. He was elected as chairman of the Committee of the Whole at the convention. This responsibility was next most important to George Washington's, who was president of the convention. Gorham had an important role in the writing of the Constitution. He strongly opposed limiting voting rights to property owners, as some favored. According to Madison, Gorham told the convention, "The people have been long accustomed to this right in various parts of America, and will never allow it to be abridged. We must consult their rooted prejudices if we expect their concurrence in our propositions."[5] On the last day of the convention, just before the signing of the Constitution, Gorham moved that there be one representative for every 30,000 rather than every 40,000. George Washington favored the motion—one of the few times he spoke up during the almost four months—and the motion passed. Like several others, Gorham believed that money was to be made on western land speculation. He lost his fortune and died at age fifty-eight, largely from worry over financial losses.

Rufus King (32) was a general's aide in the Revolutionary War and subsequently helped draft the Constitution. After the war, he finished a degree at Harvard and became a prominent lawyer. He was elected to the Massachusetts legislature and represented his state in the Confederation Congress and later the Constitutional Convention. During the convention, he favored a strong national government. He was an ardent spokesman for the large northern states and strongly opposed slavery. He served in both the Committee of Detail and the Committee on Style, thereby influencing the language of the document. He fought for its ratification.

King was twice the Federalist Party's candidate for vice-president and once for president. He served in government positions under six presidents, twice as U.S. minister to Great Britain, and twice as a U.S. senator.

Connecticut

William Samuel Johnson (59), a leading lawyer and brilliant educator, received a master of arts degree from both Yale and Harvard and an honorary doctor of laws degree from Oxford. Johnson originally disapproved of American independence and worked to preserve the relationship between Great Britain and the colonies. He declined election as a delegate at the first Continental Congress because he did not believe that the colonies should separate from Great Britain. As the war came to a close, he was again elected to the Continental Congress. He was one of the leading supporters of the "Connecticut Compromise" or "Great Compromise" that saved the convention proceedings. He presided over the Committee on Style, which drafted the final document.

During ratification in Connecticut, he appealed, "Though no enthusiast, I cannot but impute it to a signal intervention of divine providence, that a convention of states differing in circumstances, interests, and manners, should be so harmonious in adopting one grand system."[6]

Johnson simultaneously served as first president of Columbia University and United States senator.

Roger Sherman (66) is the only man who signed four of America's greatest documents: the Articles of Association of the Congress of 1774, the First Continental Congress; the Declaration of Independence; the Articles of Confederation; and the Constitution. He had thirty years' experience as a lawyer and legislator when he took his seat at the Constitutional Convention. He took part in many of the debates and helped to structure the "Connecticut Compromise."

A fellow delegate said of Sherman, "No man has a better heart nor a clearer head." He had a reputation for honest common sense and was strongly opposed to slavery, regarding it as "iniquitous." He supported a national government with limited powers, and when the Constitution was completed, he worked for its ratification in the state of Connecticut. He subsequently served as a member of Congress and as a U.S. senator.

New York

Alexander Hamilton (30 or 32) fought at Long Island, White Plains, Trenton, Princeton, and Yorktown during the War of Revolution. He was subsequently promoted as Washington's chief aide at age twenty. He was later elected by the New York legislature to the Congress of Confederation, where he met James Madison and Robert Morris.

During the convention, he favored a strong national government and presented a plan with a hereditary monarch. After fellow delegates rejected his view that the British form of government was the "best in the world," Hamilton left the convention and did not return until August. He urged delegates to sign the finished document by observing that no one's ideas were more remote from the plan than his, but that the alternative was anarchy.

Hamilton's most significant contribution was made while the Constitution awaited ratification. He collaborated with Madison and Jay in writing the *Federalist Papers,* considered the greatest treatise on federalism ever written in this country. Hamilton and Madison turned out eighty of the eighty-five essays in just six months. Hamilton was the chief contributor.

As the first secretary of the treasury under Washington, Hamilton brought the country from financial disaster. He was subsequently shot in a duel with Aaron Burr and died the next day.

New Jersey

William Livingston (63) was a member of the powerful and wealthy Livingston family. He fought during the revolution and later won fame for his political essays. He took into his household a homeless sixteen-year-old boy and put the boy through school, an act of kindness that greatly affected American history. The boy was Alexander Hamilton.

Livingston served in the Second Continental Congress. As governor of the state of New Jersey, he was elected as delegate to the Philadelphia Convention. Although he could not participate in all the sessions because of his duties as governor, he represented the small states. He subsequently urged New Jersey to ratify the new Constitution.

Livingston served eleven times as governor of New Jersey.

William Paterson (42) graduated from College of New Jersey (now Princeton) in law at age seventeen. He was the leading speaker for the small states, having authored the New Jersey Plan, which called for maintaining the present Articles of Confederation. William Pierce wrote of him: "[Paterson] is a man of great modesty, with looks that bespeak no great talents, but he is a classic, a lawyer and an orator—and of a disposition so favorable to his advancement that every one seemed ready to exalt him with their praises."[7]

He served as governor of New Jersey, U. S. senator, and associate justice of the Supreme Court.

David Brearley (42) served as lieutenant colonel in the Revolutionary War. He was admitted to the bar in New Jersey at age twenty-one. An outspoken patriot, he was arrested for treason but was freed by friends. He was elected by the state legislature as chief justice of New Jersey. An ardent Episcopalian, he helped compile *The Book of Common Prayer.*

During the Convention, Brearley strongly opposed the plan of the large states for disproportionate representation. He was a strong supporter of the new Constitution. After Washington's election as president, he was appointed as district judge of New Jersey.

Jonathan Dayton (26) was the youngest delegate to sign the Constitution. He graduated from Princeton at age fifteen and served a distinguished military career as an officer during the revolution. He did not take his seat in the convention until nearly a month after the proceedings had begun.

William Pierce described him as a person of talents "with ambition to exert them." He also said he had "an impetuosity in his temper that is injurious to him." Dayton later urged ratification of the Constitution in New Jersey.

Dayton was elected to Congress five times and served as

speaker of the house. He served as United States senator from New Jersey from 1799 to 1805. He was later indicted for treason because of his association with Aaron Burr, but he was never brought to trial. Thè city of Dayton, Ohio, is named after him.

Pennsylvania

Benjamin Franklin (81), the oldest to sign the Constitution, had the greatest number of years in diplomatic service. He was one of the original signers of the Declaration of Independence. His infirmities precluded active participation in the convention, but his presence and prestige added dignity and weight to the results. Moreover, his humor placated harsh feelings. At one seeming impasse, he petitioned for prayer. William Pierce wrote of him, "He is no Speaker, nor does he seem to let politics engage his attention. He is, however, a most extraordinary man, and tells a story in a style more engaging than anything I have ever heard."[8]

Franklin's ideas for government were quite dissimilar to the final results of the Convention. He favored a unicameral (one house) legislature and an executive council comprised of several members rather than a single executive. But even though his ideas were not incorporated into the document, he strongly favored the new federal government and urged the delegates to sign the Constitution.

Thomas FitzSimons (46) was the first Roman Catholic to be elected to public office in Pennsylvania. He served as an officer in the Revolutionary War and later served as a delegate to the Congress of Confederation. As a delegate to the Constitutional Convention, he favored property ownership for voting in congressional elections. He later served as a member of the first House of Representatives in 1789.

Thomas Mifflin (43) was Washington's first aide-de-camp in the Revolutionary War. Mifflin's military career, however, was tainted. While serving as quartermaster, he was compelled to resign because of suspicion of misappropriated funds.

Mifflin served as president of the Congress of

Confederation that elected Washington as the commander
of the Continental Army.

Mifflin was elected to the Constitutional Convention but
took little part in the debates except to sign the document.
He served three three-year terms as governor from 1790 to
1799. After his last term as governor, Mifflin was appointed
as commander in chief of the Philadelphia militia. He also
served the last months of his life in the Philadelphia House
of Representatives. During the political campaign, he was
accused of defalcation of public funds.

Jared Ingersoll (38) was a graduate from Yale at age
sixteen. He studied law in England, where he became a supporter of the American cause. He became a distinguished
lawyer and later served as attorney general of Pennsylvania.
He apparently did not take part in the debates at the convention. However, Madison noted in his journal that Ingersoll
supported Franklin's motion to sign the Constitution. "Mr.
Ingersoll," Madison wrote, "did not consider the signing
either as a mere attestation of the fact . . . but as a recom-
mendation of what . . . was the most eligible."9

He was later an unsuccessful candidate for the vice-
presidency on the Federalist party ticket. He died a poor
man because of his land speculation.

Robert Morris (53), large and good-humored, was one of
the country's wealthiest men. He was one of seven delegates
to the Convention who were also signers of the Declaration
of Independence. He pledged his credit for supplies during
the Revolutionary War, earning him the title "Financier of
the Revolution." He was a constant companion to Washington and nominated Washington as president of the convention. Morris favored strong central government and said of
the new Constitution: "Some have boasted [the Constitu-
tion] as a work from Heaven, others have given it a less
righteous origin. I have many reasons to believe it is the
work of plain, honest men."10 Morris served in the U. S.
Senate from 1789-1795. He subsequently lost his fortune on
land speculation and served a term in debtors prison.

James Wilson (44), an original signer of the Declaration

of Independence, was considered one of the most learned men at the convention. Educated in Scotland, he had studied every revolution in history and helped frame the judicial language of the document. Wilson favored proportional representation in both the House and the Senate but was strongly opposed to wealth as a criterion for representation. Because of Franklin's poor health, Wilson frequently read his speeches during the convention. Speaking with a Scotch burr, Wilson was able to persuade others of the need for a national government. A fellow delegate said that "he draws the attention not by the charm of his eloquence, but by the force of his reasoning."[11] Wilson served as an associate justice of the Supreme Court. He wrote that "all power is derived from the people—that their happiness is the end of government."

George Clymer (48), a banker, was also a signer of the Declaration of Independence and later a member of the Continental Congress. He successfully opposed Alexander Hamilton's plan for ratification that the Congress of the Confederation should approve the new Constitution before sending it to the individual states for ratification. After the Constitution's ratification, Clymer served as a representative in the first congress.

Gouverneur Morris (35), lawyer and accomplished orator, gave more speeches during the convention than any other in his advocacy of a strong central government. The elegance of the language in the Constitution is attributable to Morris. He wrote much of the final draft and is credited with its preamble. Madison wrote of him: "The finish given to the style and arrangement of the Constitution, fairly belongs to the pen of Mr. Morris."[12] He attended Kings College (now Columbia University) and later studied law. He was admitted to the bar at age twenty. He was a signer of the Articles of Confederation. When some of the delegates in 1776 hesitated on declaring independence, the twenty-four-year-old Morris made an impassioned speech. In the course of his speech he said: "We have no business with the King. We did not quarrel with the King. He has officiously made himself a party in the dispute against us. And now he pretends to be the umpire. Trust crocodiles, trust the hungry wolf in your flock, or a rattlesnake in your bosom, you may yet be something wise. But trust the King, his ministers, his commissioners, it is madness in the extreme!"[13]

Morris originated the American decimal coinage system and later served as U. S. minister to France during the French Revolution. Elected as a United States senator, Morris strongly urged the purchase of Louisiana as a means of ridding the territory of Napoleon's rule.

Delaware

George Read (53) was admitted to the bar at age nineteen. He served as a delegate to the Continental Congress. Initially opposing independence from Great Britain, he later signed the declaration at the peril of his personal fortune. During the convention, he advocated a strong central government that would abolish the states. He was also an effective representative for the small states and fought to preserve their vote.

Because of his influence, Delaware was the first state to ratify the Constitution. On the last day of the convention, Read signed the Constitution and also signed proxy for John Dickinson, his close boyhood friend.

Read later served as U. S. senator and as chief justice of Delaware.

Richard Bassett (42) helped found the Methodist Church in the United States. He later became a Methodist lay preacher. He served as a captain in the Revolutionary War. Educated as a lawyer, he favored strong central government. He played an important role in getting Delaware to ratify the Constitution. He was elected as U. S. senator from Delaware and was one of eight members who drew up the bill that established the federal court system of the United States. Bassett served as governor of Delaware and was later appointed U. S. district court judge by President Thomas Jefferson.

Gunning Bedford, Jr. (40), a lawyer, was an aide-de-camp to Washington during the Revolutionary War. He was a classmate of James Madison at Princeton. He was one of the most outspoken of the delegates for the interests of the smaller states. With Bassett and Read, he was influential in persuading Delaware's convention to ratify the Constitution. President George Washington appointed Bedford as the first U. S. district court judge for Delaware, a position he occupied till his death.

John Dickinson (54), a Quaker, studied law in England and was called the "penman of the Revolution" because of the many historic documents he wrote. He wrote the "Petition to the King," which was adopted by the Continental Congress in 1774, and the famed essay "Declaration of Rights and Grievances of the Colonists of America," which challenged the British right to tax the colonies. He also penned the "Declaration on the Causes and Necessity of Taking Up Arms" in 1775. He served as a legislator both in Delaware and Pennsylvania.

Dickinson served in the Continental Congress and is credited with drafting the Articles of Confederation. He also signed the document. He refused to sign the Declaration of Independence because he believed that the British people would recognize the folly of Parliament's actions toward the colonists. He was a strong defender for the rights of small states. His advocacy that the House of Representatives should be elected by the people and the Senate by the state legislatures was the basis for the Great Compromise. Unable to attend the signing of the Constitution, he authorized George Read to sign for him by proxy. At his death, Thomas Jefferson said, "A more estimable man or truer patriot could not have left us."

Jacob Broom (35) was a financier. His major contribution during the convention was his appeal that delegates *must* agree on a new plan of government, even if by a bare majority. The convention was on the verge of breaking up when Broom made his appeal, and it seemed to have the effect of causing the convention to proceed. He was a member of the Delaware legislature for five years.

Maryland

James McHenry (33), a physician who had fought during the revolution, was an aide to Washington. He was subsequently taken as a prisoner of war by the British. After his release he became the senior surgeon at Valley Forge army hospital.

McHenry served as a representative from Maryland to the Congress of Confederation. He was also a delegate to the Constitutional Convention but attended only about half the sessions. Even though he had some reservations about parts of the Constitution, McHenry signed it, urged its ratification, and remained an ardent Federalist the rest of his life. He was appointed by Washington and Adams as secretary of war. Fort McHenry in Maryland was named after him.

Daniel Carroll (56), a wealthy landowner, merchant, and Roman Catholic, signed both the Articles of Confederation and the Constitution. He was a delegate to the Continental Congress. He replaced his cousin, Charles Carroll, a signer of the Declaration of Independence, at the Constitutional Convention. He defended the new government provided by the Constitution as the "best form of government which has ever been offered to the world." He was a strong advocate for a national government and urged Maryland to ratify the document. He was elected to the first Congress as a representative from Maryland.

Daniel of St. Thomas Jenifer (64) was a wealthy landowner, bachelor, aristocrat, and friend of Washington. He was a delegate in the Continental Congress and later served during the Revolutionary War. He subsequently served as a substitute delegate when one of four men from Maryland refused to serve. He took little part in the debates at the convention, but after he signed, he urged Maryland's ratification.

Virginia

John Blair (55) was described by a fellow delegate, William Pierce, as "one of the most respectable men in Virginia, both on account of his family as well as fortune. . . .

His good sense, and most excellent principles, compensate for other deficiencies."[14]

He graduated from William and Mary College and studied law at Middle Temple in London. He was appointed to Virginia's general court at age forty-six and later became its chief judge. He was one of three Virginians (the other two were Washington and Madison) who signed the Constitution. He subsequently opposed Patrick Henry and spoke out in favor of the Constitution at Virginia's ratifying convention.

James Madison, Jr. (36), sometimes referred to as the "Father of the Constitution," possessed a profound knowledge of government and formulated the plan for the large states. Madison received his education at Princeton University, whose president was the Reverend John Witherspoon, a signer of the Declaration. Witherspoon introduced Madison to the Scottish philosophers, the most prominent of which was David Hume. Madison helped draft the Virginian constitution. He also helped organize the government under the Articles of Confederation.

As a delegate to the convention, Madison kept the most complete record of the proceedings in his "Notes on Debate." William Pierce said of him, "He always comes forward as the best informed man of any point in debate." Madison spoke the most often during the debates. Pierce also observed that "every Person seems to acknowledge his greatness. He blends together the profound politician with the Scholar . . . and tho' he cannot be called an Orator, he is a most agreeable, eloquent and convincing Speaker. . . . The affairs of the United States, he perhaps, has the most correct knowledge of, of any man in the Union."[15] Madison later joined with Hamilton and Jay in authoring the *Federalist Papers.* He wrote of the Constitution in essay 37, "It is impossible for the man of pious reflection not to perceive in it a finger of that Almighty hand which has been so frequently and signally extended to our relief in the critical stages of the revolution."

He introduced the amendments to the Constitution that

became the Bill of Rights. He served as a member of Congress, as secretary of state, and as fourth president of the United States. He lived to age eighty-five, longer than any of the Founding Fathers from the time of the signing of the Constitution.

North Carolina

William Blount (38), born wealthy, was seemingly more interested in using his office for power than in serving his constituency. He was later found guilty of fraud and bribery in achieving his ends. Blount had served as a member of the Continental Congress. While serving as a member of the North Carolina legislature, he acquired immense wealth through devious land speculations.

During the convention, Blount was not particularly involved nor interested and stayed in Philadelphia only the first two weeks. He later returned in August and remained through the signing. He later claimed his signature did not mean that he agreed to the Constitution, only that he was present. His motive for a strong central government was to enhance his western lands development. Although he worked for ratification of the Constitution, the North Carolina legislature was controlled by Antifederalists, and they rejected ratification.

Blount was later appointed governor of the Territory of the United States south of the Ohio River, which gave him innumerable opportunities to enhance his land speculations. Blount later won statehood for the territory and was elected as Tennessee's first senator. Blount's friends were subsequently exposed before Congress, and the U. S. House of Representatives voted to impeach him. The next day he was expelled by the U. S. Senate for conspiracy and land fraud.

Hugh Williamson (51), physician, was an outstanding scholar and scientist. He served in the Revolutionary War as surgeon general. He was one of the most educated men in the convention. He was in the first graduating class of the University of Pennsylvania. His postgraduate studies included ordination to the Presbyterian ministry, a master's degree in mathematics, and a doctorate in medicine from the University of Utrecht (Netherlands). He took up the practice of medicine at age thirty-two. Because of a scientific paper he published in astronomy, Williamson received a doctor of laws degree from the University of Leyden.

He was elected by North Carolina to the Congress of Confederation. Thomas Jefferson said of him, "I found him a very useful member, of an acute mind, attentive to business, and of an high degree of erudition."[16]

When the convention appeared deadlocked, Williamson urged, "If we do not concede on both sides, our business must soon be at an end." He was the first to suggest that a United States senator serve a term of six years—a proposition that eventually became part of the Constitution.

Williamson became the first representative from North Carolina to the U. S. Congress.

Richard Dobbs Spaight (29) served as lieutenant colonel during the Revolutionary War. He represented North Carolina to the Congress of Confederation and was later elected by the legislature to the Constitutional Convention. Spaight was the first to advocate that senators should be chosen by state legislators, a provision in the original Constitution that remained in effect till the seventeenth amendment.

After the convention, Spaight was elected governor, serving till 1795. He was elected as a representative to Congress in 1798. He was one of three of the founders who died in duels as a result of politics. He died at age forty-four.

South Carolina

John Rutledge (48) was South Carolina's leading citizen and a distinguished lawyer whose legal knowledge was used in drafting the Constitution. Rutledge had studied law at Middle Temple in London. At age twenty-five, he was appointed attorney general of South Carolina. He was a delegate to the first and second continental congresses. As a delegate to the Constitutional Convention, Rutledge had a leading role representing the slave states. After the Constitution was approved, he led the South Carolina delegation in urging ratification.

Rutledge was named associate justice of the Supreme

Court but never attended any sessions. He resigned his position in 1791 to accept the appointment of Chief Justice of the Supreme Court of South Carolina. He was later appointed Chief Justice of the Supreme Court in 1795, but the Senate refused to confirm the appointment.

Charles Pinckney (29), the son of a wealthy plantation owner and lawyer, received his education in England, where he commenced his legal training at Middle Temple in London at age fifteen. During the War of Revolution, he was captured by the British and remained a prisoner till the end of the war. He was a member of the Congress of Confederation and was later elected by the state legislature to the Constitutional Convention. During the convention, he authored the so-called "Pinckney Plan," a copy of which has never been discovered. Historians are generally agreed that he was responsible for many provisions in the drafted Constitution. He worked for the ratification of the Constitution in South Carolina, declaring that it was better calculated "to answer the ends of public happiness" than any other form of government.

Pinckney was a cousin to Charles Cotesworth Pinckney. He was four times elected governor of South Carolina, a United States senator, a member of Congress, and United States minister to Spain.

Charles Cotesworth Pinckney (41) was one of the most highly educated of the delegates to the convention. He spent sixteen years at schools in England and France. He studied under William Blackstone, the famous professor of English law who so influenced the framers of the Constitution. During the Revolutionary War, he served as a brigadier general, was captured by the British, and, like his cousin Charles, was taken prisoner. When the British taunted him, he replied, "My heart is altogether American, and neither severity, nor favor, nor poverty, nor affluence can ever induce me to swerve from it." Pinckney was later appointed major general and third in command in the new U. S. Army from 1798 to 1800.

Pinckney's extensive legal background was used in

drafting the Constitution. While serving as an envoy to France, he exposed the diplomatic blackmail of the United States by French envoys as a price for their friendship. In doing so, he earned his country's admiration. Pinckney was an unsuccessful candidate for vice-president on the Federalist party ticket and was twice unsuccessful in his bid for the presidency.

Pierce Butler (42) was a strong spokesman for southern slaveholders. He advocated that the number of representatives from each state should be based on the wealth of the state, not population. He served in the South Carolina legislature almost continuously for ten years. He was a strong exponent for states' rights during the convention and opposed any plan that would diminish those rights. He opposed the concept of representation that counted each slave as three-fifths of a person, advocating that slaves ought to have the same representation as free men. He was also responsible for the clause in the Constitution that ensured that runaway slaves should be returned to their owners. Though he was an immigrant, he opposed plans for removing restrictions on immigration because immigrants brought with them foreign ideologies.

Butler urged ratification of the Constitution in South Carolina, and, after it passed, he was elected by the legislature to the Senate.

Georgia

William Few (39) was self-educated and served as a lieutenant colonel in the Revolutionary War. He was elected a delegate to the Continental Congress. He agreed with Madison that the Articles of Confederation were inadequate and favored a national government. He participated in the convention only for the first month and then went to New York to attend Congress, which was in session.

Abraham Baldwin (32) was a Yale-educated lawyer who founded the University of Georgia. Exceptionally bright, he entered Yale at age thirteen and graduated at age seventeen. At the Constitutional Convention, he favored a national

government. He regarded his service at the convention as
the crowning achievement of his career. Baldwin was
elected to the first congress. He was a member of the congressional committee that drafted the Bill of Rights. He was
later elected by the legislature in 1799 as a senator from
Georgia.

Edmund Randolph of Virginia, who introduced the
"Virginia Plan" into the convention proceedings, refused to
sign the Constitution but later warmly supported its ratification in Virginia. George Mason (Virginia) and Elbridge Gerry
(Massachusetts) also declined to sign. Ironically, Gerry
served as vice-president under the new Constitution. All
three explained that the Constitution needed amendments.
Of the twenty-six amendments to the Constitution, twelve,
including the Bill of Rights, were advocated by these three.

Although these signers were hardly the "assembly of
demigods" proclaimed by Jefferson, they were distinguished and seasoned in government affairs and were
broadly experienced in constitution-making. Their wisdom
was derived from practical experience, their guide during
the convention. The great genius of their accomplishment at
the convention was that they blended their experiences and
ideas into a document that has outlived their agrarian society.

Some twentieth-century historians, most notably
Charles Beard,[17] have imputed baser motives to the
founders, but their arguments have not held up under
scholarly scrutiny. Recent studies have shown the founders
to be men of character and virtue in the sense that they
placed the interests of the nation before personal interests,
in spite of a few exceptions.[18] The research corroborates
this statement by James Madison:

> I feel it a duty to express my profound & solemn con-
> viction, derived from my intimate opportunity of observ-
> ing & appreciating the views of the Convention, collec-
> tively & individually, that there never was an assembly of
> men, charged with a great & arduous trust, who were
> *more pure in their motives,* or more exclusively or

anxiously [devoted to the object committed to them, than were the members of the Federal Convention of 1787, to the object of devising and proposing a constitutional system which would best supply the defects of that which it was to replace, and best secure the permanent liberty and happiness of their country.][19]

3

"The Event Is in the Hand of God"

Our greatest possession is not the vast domain;
it's not our beautiful mountains, or our fertile
prairies, or our magnificent coastline. It's not the
might of our Army or Navy. These things are of
great importance. But in my judgment the greatest and most precious possession of the American
people is the Constitution.
Senator Sam Ervin

The new Constitution was a bombshell to the
states. Convention meetings had been secret.
State legislatures had sent the delegates to the
Philadelphia Convention for the "sole and express purpose of revising the Articles of Confederation." But other delegates, notably Madison and
Hamilton, came with an agenda to "devise such further provisions as shall appear to them necessary to render the constitution of the federal government adequate to the
exigencies of the Union." It is safe to say that none of the
states expected such a revolutionary course as the delegates
had taken.

When they emerged from the State House in Philadelphia after their three and a half months of deliberations, they
had a written constitution that abolished the Articles of Confederation, nullified the Continental Congress, and created a
two-tiered government—one federal to unite the new
republic, and the other state and local to keep power close
to the people. Conceived thereby was a democratic republic
that rested on an elected executive, elected members of

47

Congress to represent the people, and senators elected by the states to represent the states.

The federal government was given specific limitations to protect the people from arbitrary coercion. All powers not vested in the federal government were reserved to the states and the people. Convinced that power corrupts, the framers of the new Constitution divided the powers of the national government and provided for checks and balances. The new charter further provided for an independent judicial review of legislation, procedures for amending the Constitution, and an explicit declaration that the new Constitution was the supreme law of the land. The most extraordinary feature in the document was the declaration that the people were sovereign, not the officers of the government or its institutions.

Never before in the history of mankind had such a noble experiment in self-government been attempted. This effort was premised on the conviction and belief of the delegates that government exists to protect the citizens' rights to life, liberty, property, and pursuit of happiness.

Today we look back on the achievement of that august body and regard what they did as miraculous. But this was not the general perception of their countrymen in 1787 after they returned to their respective states. Their efforts divided the people into two opposing camps—those who supported the Constitution (the Federalists) and those who opposed (the Antifederalists). The latter group claimed that the delegates had overstepped their instructions by creating a new government and had, in effect, defied Congress. Would not such a revolutionary charter, they challenged, result in tyranny and the loss of liberty secured by the war with Britain? Would not the newly proposed government be as autocratic as the monarchy?

Earlier Experiments with Constitutionalism

The fifty-five delegates that eventually came to the Philadelphia Convention were already committed to constitu-

tionalism.[1] They were agreed that an explicit charter of laws
—a written constitution—was necessary to restrain government, guarantee rights, and be regarded as supreme law.
Their view of constitutionalism was based on the reasoning
that there were commonly accepted principles to which all
people should be subject. Constitutionalism implied that all
legislatures and judiciaries were bound by these general
principles that must guide their actions in securing the rights
of individuals. When legislative acts encroach on the
people's rights, a petition for judicial review would ascertain
whether the act was constitutional or subject to repudia-
tion.[2]

The experiment with constitutionalism was not new to
the delegates. Forty-two of them had belonged to the Continental Congress, and most had helped draft the Articles of
Confederation and their respective state constitutions. The
British constitutional system, which consisted of laws, cus-
toms, and legal precedents established by Parliament, was
regarded as unworkable in satisfying the colonists' claims
against Parliament. They therefore concluded that there had
to be a fixed constitution to protect themselves against arbitrary action.

The Declaration of Independence severed the country
from Great Britain but did not specify the type of governmental system that would replace colonial dependency on
the monarchy. In fact, as Garry Wills has pointed out, not
one country, but thirteen separate ones, came into existence
when the declaration was made unanimous in July 1776.
The second Continental Congress addressed the problem of
a union of states in 1777 and established the first written
constitution of the United States called "The Articles of Confederation and Perpetual Union." But this document was
not ratified by the states until four years later—March 1,
1781.[3] Six years after ratification, it was discovered that the
articles were not practical.

The Articles of Confederation provided for a "firm
league of friendship" between the states and for their

"common defense, the security of the liberties, and their mutual and general welfare," but it also had serious defects.

The articles provided a national congress but no executive or judicial branch. Sovereignty was left completely to the states. This made the confederation powerless to make the states comply with its resolutions. The major problem under the Articles of Confederation was that Congress had no power to levy taxes and, consequently, could not pay its bills. In effect, Congress could do nothing without approval by two-thirds of the states. The result was that problems that arose between the states, principally over interstate trade and commerce, were not adjudicated. When Daniel Shays, a Revolutionary War veteran, led a revolt in Massachusetts, it seemed to presage what many feared—insurrection and anarchy.

Washington registered his alarm in these words: "It is indispensable to the happiness of the individual States, that there should be lodged somewhere, a Supreme Power to regulate and govern the general concerns of the Confederated Republic, without which the Union cannot be of long duration."[4] He later wrote, "The fabrick which took nine years, at the expense of much blood and treasure, to rear, now totters to the foundation, and without support must soon fall."[5] James Madison echoed the same concern in a letter he wrote to Edmund Randolph, governor of Virginia: "Our situation is becoming every day more and more critical. . . . People of reflection unanimously agree that the existing Confederacy is tottering to its foundation."[6]

The historian John Fiske called this period "the most critical moment in all the history of the American people." Congress recognized the severity of the crisis and approved the calling of a convention in 1787 for the purpose of revising the Articles of Confederation. The selected site was Independence Hall in Philadelphia, where the declaration was signed and adopted. In that time, Philadelphia was the most cosmopolitan city of the states with a population of slightly less than 30,000.

The Constitutional Convention

Seventy-four delegates were appointed by their state legislatures to the convention, but the most that came was fifty-five. Twelve of the thirteen states were represented. Rhode Island boycotted the convention because the state wanted to protect its economic interests from a national government.

The delegates came from different backgrounds, and their divergent views often clashed during the heated summer days. In the end, however, they put aside cherished personal views and made concessions in the interest of a federal union. How these delegates decided on establishing a federal government rather than a federation of states as it existed under the Articles of Confederation is a remarkable story.

The Convention was to have started on May 14, but a quorum of states was not assembled until May 25. The Virginia delegation used the intervening time to draft a plan, the fundamentals of which were to form the new federal constitution.

The convention's first order of business was to select a presiding officer. George Washington was unanimously elected. With characteristic self-effacement, he accepted the responsibility. Before a full quorum had arrived, there had been talk about approving measures that would be acceptable to the people. Washington was reported to have said, "It is probable that no plan we propose will be adopted. Perhaps another dreadful conflict is to be sustained. If to please the people we offer what we ourselves disapprove, how can we afterwards defend our work. Let us raise a standard to which the wise and honest can repair. The event is in the hand of God."[7]

James Madison chose a seat in front of the presiding officer and recorded the secret convention proceedings. Were it not for his meticulous notes on the convention, knowledge of the debates would be scant.[8]

On May 29, Governor Edmund Randolph from Virginia

presented the Virginia Plan to the convention. The plan, drafted by Madison and containing fifteen resolutions, represented the views of the larger states. It called for a national legislature comprised of two houses based on population. The lower house, elected by the people, was to elect the upper chamber. The national legislature had veto power over the acts of state legislatures whenever the "articles of union" were violated. Congress further had power to compel the states to obedience. The plan also called for a "national executive" elected by both houses and a "national judiciary." The executive and a portion of the judiciary had veto power over legislation by Congress. This executive and judiciary review was empowered to ensure that each state would have a republican form of government. Within this plan was the germ of ideas that were later adopted in the Constitution.

The Virginia Plan was given to a Committee of the Whole. After thirteen sessions, the committee reported to the convention their approval of an amended Virginia Plan that called for a single executive who had veto power and was chosen by the legislature. Also recommended was the election of the upper house by state legislatures.

While the Committee of the Whole was meeting, delegates from New Jersey developed an alternative plan that represented the small states. On June 15, William Paterson countered with the New Jersey Plan to the convention, which was little more than a revised Articles of Confederation. It called for a plural executive, a supreme court, and for giving Congress power to levy duty taxes on imports, to regulate commerce, and to collect taxes. It also provided for an oath by state officials to compel support to the national government, and it specified the supremacy of the Union in its sphere.

Both plans were debated in committee for several days. The small states argued against a national government on the basis that the convention was called only to amend the Articles of Confederation. The larger states argued that the convention had the right to propose whatever was in the best interests of the union. During this debate, Hamilton made a novel proposal that the convention adopt a government based on the British system with a monarch and senate elected for life. The committee quickly dismissed the proposal because it was too similar to the hereditary nobility concept of the British. Hamilton left the convention several days later only to return for brief visits and to sign the final document.

After three days debate on the Virginia and New Jersey plans, the committee voted seven to three on June 19 for an amended Virginia Plan. Thus the convention decided to approve a national government based on an independent, bicameral legislature; a national judiciary; and one executive.

After spending several days on minor details, the convention moved to resolve the most important issue—how representation in the legislature would be determined. The debates were heated and intense. Madison had previously said to the convention: "The great difficulty lies in the affair of Representation; and if this could be adjusted, all others would be surmountable."[9]

The issue was between the larger and smaller states. The smaller states wanted equal representation. The larger states wanted representation proportional to size. The convention appeared deadlocked. At that juncture, Benjamin Franklin, too weak to speak, wrote out a proposal for his colleague, James Wilson, to read:

> The small progress we have made after 4 or five weeks . . . is methinks a melancholy proof of the imperfection of the Human Understanding. We indeed seem to feel our own want of political wisdom, since we have been running about in search of it. . . . In this situation . . . groping as it were in the dark to find political truth . . . how has it happened, Sir, that we have not hitherto once thought of humbly applying to the Father of lights to illuminate our understandings? . . . I have lived, Sir, a long time, and the longer I live, the more convincing proofs I see of this truth—*that God Governs in the affairs of men.* And if a sparrow cannot fall to the ground

without his notice, is it probable that an empire can rise
without his aid?

We have been assured, Sir, in the sacred writings, that
"except the Lord build the House they labour in vain that
build it." I firmly believe this; and I also believe that
without his concurring aid we shall succeed in this political building no better, than the Builders of Babel: We shall
be divided by our little partial local interests; our projects
will be confounded, and we ourselves shall become a re-
proach and bye word down to future ages. And what is
worse, mankind may hereafter from this unfortunate instance, despair of establishing Governments by Human
wisdom and leave it to chance, war, and conquest.

I therefore beg leave to move—that henceforth
prayers imploring the assistance of Heaven, and its blessings on our deliberations, be held in this Assembly every
morning before we proceed to business, and that one or
more of the Clergy of this City be requested to officiate in
that Service.[10]

Most historians agree that Franklin's motion was not
acted on since the convention lacked funds for a chaplain.
But his appeal had altered the mood of the convention. He
further appealed for more conciliation between the larger
and smaller states: "When a broad table is to be made, and
the edges of planks do not fit, the artist takes a little from
both, and makes a good joint. In like manner here both sides
must part with some of their demands, in order that they
may join in some accommodating proposition."[11]

The issue of representation was finally resolved in mid-
July with the first great compromise. The delegates eventually approved a proposal by Roger Sherman of Connecticut that representation in the lower house would be
determined by popular election and based on population of
free citizens plus three-fifths of the slaves. The upper house
(Senate) had equal representation, with two members from
each state, elected by the state legislatures. Without this
compromise, it is doubtful there would have been a federal
constitution as we now know it.

A second compromise occurred over the institution of

slavery. Madison wrote that the real "difference of interests
. . . lay not between the large & small [states], but the
[Northern] & [Southern] States" on the institution of
slavery.[12] The issue was whether slaves should be counted
for the purpose of taxation and representation in the
national Congress. The South wanted them counted for
representation purposes but objected to being taxed for
slaves. It was finally decided that three-fifths of the slaves
would be counted for both purposes.[13]

The slavery issue came up again over the regulation of
interstate commerce and trade—how importation of slaves
would be regulated among the Southern States. Out of this
debate came another compromise when the convention
decided that Congress would have power to regulate foreign
commerce but would be forbidden to abolish importation
of slaves till 1808, giving the South time to build its supply
of slaves.

The delegates next turned their attention to a discussion
of the executive branch. The divergent views during the
course of the convention had ranged from Hamilton's
monarch-elected-for-life proposal to dividing the office
among three men elected for a short time. Questions centered on how the chief executive should be elected, how
long his tenure should be, and whether the central
government should be weak or strong. Those who favored
a strong single executive wanted him elected directly by the
people as a counterbalance to the powers of Congress.
Those favoring a weak executive wanted him chosen by
Congress.

The final compromise, after weeks of discussion and
debate within committees, was that a single executive
would be elected for four-year terms with eligibility for re-
election. He was to be selected by a unique device—an
electoral college—where each state was allowed as many
electors as it had senators and congressmen in the national
legislature. The Constitution originally provided that the
person receiving the highest number of votes from the electoral college would be president; the person with the

second largest majority would be vice-president. But no provision was made for determining which of the two men was voted on for president and vice-president.[14]

There was minimal debate over the judicial branch. Early in the convention, the delegates decided that the members of the court would have a lifetime tenure. The delegates were committed to the principle of an independent review by the judiciary. Congress was further empowered to create a lower federal court system, accomplished in 1789 when it passed the Judiciary Act, which provided for appeals from state courts to the Supreme Court.

Another vital decision of the convention was that the laws and treaties of the United States government were to be the supreme law of the land, which all judges at every level were bound to enforce. The Constitution itself was declared to be the supreme law of the land. This decision made the states subservient to a national government.

Once these major issues were decided, the finer points were turned over to committees of detail and style. Gouverneur Morris drafted the preamble and was largely responsible for the Constitution's style. The document was finally presented to the convention on September 13. Washington's letter transmitted to the Congress the newly framed Constitution. After noting the need for a stronger central government and the difficulty in attaining this without sacrificing individual liberties, Washington wrote:

> In all our deliberations on this subject we kept steadily in our view, that which appears to us the greatest interest of every true American, the consolidation of our Union, in which is involved our prosperity, felicity, safety, perhaps our national existence. This important consideration, seriously and deeply impressed on our minds, led each State in the Convention to be less rigid on points of inferior magnitude, than might have been otherwise expected; and thus the Constitution, which we now present, is the result of a spirit of amity, and of that mutual deference and concession which the peculiarity of our political situation rendered indispensable.[15]

On Saturday, September 15, the delegates voted on the approval of the Constitution as amended. Madison recorded, "On the question to agree to the Constitution, as amended. All the States ay. The Constitution was then ordered to be engrossed. And the House adjourned."[16]

Finally, on September 17, 1787, the delegates signed the document. Of the fifty-five delegates that had come to the convention, only forty-one remained. Thirty-eight signed the document, and George Read signed proxy for the name of the thirty-ninth—John Dickinson from Delaware. Three delegates (George Mason, Elbridge Gerry, and Edmund Randolph) refused to sign.

Before the document was signed, Benjamin Franklin was requested to give his endorsing approval. In his speech, read by James Wilson, Franklin, in part, wrote:

> In these sentiments, Sir, I agree to this Constitution with all its faults, if they are such; because I think a general Government necessary for us, and there is no form of Government but what may be a blessing to the people if well administered, and believe farther that this is likely to be well administered for a course of years, and can only end in Despotism, as other forms have done before it, when the people shall become so corrupted as to need despotic Government, being incapable of any other. . . .
> It therefore astonishes me, Sir, to find this system approaching so near to perfection as it does; and I think it will astonish our enemies, who are waiting with confidence to hear that our councils are confounded like those of the Builders of Babel; and that our States are on the point of separation, only to meet hereafter for the purpose of cutting one another's throats. Thus I consent, Sir, to this Constitution because I expect no better, and because I am not sure, that it is not the best. The opinions I have had of its errors, I sacrifice to the public good. . . . I hope therefore that for our own sakes as a part of the people, and for the sake of posterity, we shall act heartily and unanimously in recommending this Constitution . . . wherever our influence may extend, and turn our future thoughts & endeavors to the means of having it well administered.

Summary of the 1787
Constitutional Convention Proceedings

May 25, 1787	Washington was elected as the presiding officer of the convention.
May 29, 1787	The Virginia delegation submitted to the convention fifteen propositions as a plan of government.
May 30, 1787	The convention went into a Committee of the Whole, which permitted less formal discussion, on the fifteen propositions of the Virginia Plan. Nathaniel Gorham became the chairman of the Committee of the Whole.
June 13, 1787	The Committee of the Whole reported to the convention an amended version of the Virginia Plan.
June 14, 1787	New Jersey requested an adjournment to allow the smaller states, dissatisfied with the Virginia Plan, to prepare an alternative plan. The request was granted.
June 15, 1787	New Jersey submitted nine resolutions that amended the Articles of Confederation. Vigorous debate ensued on the two plans.
June 19, 1787	The convention rejected the New Jersey Plan and voted to discuss the Virginia Plan. The small states threatened withdrawal. Franklin appealed to the convention for prayer (June 28).

July 2, 1787	Convention was deadlocked on the question of each state having an equal vote for the Senate. The matter was referred to a committee of eleven.
July 5, 1787	The committee of eleven submitted its report to the convention; this report became the basis for the Great Compromise.
July 24, 1787	The fifteen Virginia Resolutions had been expanded to twenty-three in the previous debates. A committee of five (Rutledge, Randolph, Gorham, Ellsworth, and Wilson) were appointed as a Committee on Detail to draft a constitution from the resolutions.
August 6-10, 1787	The report of the Committee on Detail was discussed clause by clause. Amendments and compromises were made.
September 8, 1787	Another committee of five (Johnson, Hamilton, Gouverneur Morris, Madison, and King) were appointed as a Committee on Style to revise the document and arrange its contents.
September 12, 1787	The report of the Committee on Style was printed.
September 15, 1787	The Constitution was ordered engrossed.
September 17, 1787	The Constitution was signed by thirty-nine of the forty-two delegates.

> On the whole, Sir, I cannot help expressing a wish
> that every member of the Convention who may still have
> objections to it, would with me, on this occasion doubt a
> little of his own infallibility, and to make manifest our
> unanimity, put his name to this instrument.[17]

While the last members were signing, Madison recorded
that Benjamin Franklin looked toward the president's chair,
the back of which had a painting of a rising sun. Franklin
observed that painters had found it difficult to distinguish
between a rising and a setting sun. "I have," said he, "often
and often in the course of the Session, and the vicissitudes
of my hopes and fears as to its issue, looked at that [sun]
behind the President without being able to tell whether it
was rising or setting: But now at length I have the happiness
to know that it is a rising and not a setting Sun."[18]

Ratification of the Constitution

Considering that the Articles of Confederation had taken
five years to approve, the delegates realistically understood
that it would be difficult to obtain the Confederation
Congress's approval for a document that nullified the congress's existence. They also realized that state legislators pre-
dominantly supported "states rights" and would therefore
be reluctant to approve a national charter. So the convention decided upon a revolutionary method of ratification.
They took the document directly to the states' ratifying
conventions, a decision that was tantamount to taking it
directly to the people. They further specified that nine of
the thirteen states would be sufficient to establish the Constitution. The decision proved to be ingenious because it
worked and eliminated prolonged debate.

Ratification of the Constitution took only nine months,
but the controversy over the new charter was intense.
Before the delegates returned to their states, Richard Henry
Lee denounced it in Congress. Patrick Henry, George
Mason, and James Monroe opposed it in Virginia. Governor
George Clinton opposed it in New York. Lines were quickly

Order in Which the States Ratified
the Constitution

1. Delaware	December 7, 1787
2. Pennsylvania	December 12, 1787
3. New Jersey	December 19, 1787
4. Georgia	January 2, 1788
5. Connecticut	January 9, 1788
6. Massachusetts	February 6, 1788
7. Maryland	April 28, 1788
8. South Carolina	May 23, 1788
9. New Hampshire	June 21, 1788
10. Virginia	June 25, 1788
11. New York	July 26, 1788

(The Continental Congress passed a resolution on September 13, 1788, that put the new Constitution into operation.)

12. North Carolina (voted not to ratify the new Constitution after its first convention, but then ratified at the second convention)	November 21, 1789
13. Rhode Island (did not call a convention but when the new government came into operation and Rhode Island was in danger of being regarded as a foreign government, it called a convention and ratified)	May 29, 1790

drawn between those who opposed (Antifederalists) and those who favored (Federalists).

A major objection against the Constitution was that it lacked a specific bill of rights. John Adams and Thomas Jefferson, both of whom were out of the country during the convention, deplored this omission, even though they generally favored the document. Jefferson wrote to Madison, "A bill of rights is what the people are entitled to against every government on earth, . . . and what no government should refuse."[19]

Delaware ratified the Constitution just less than three months after the document was signed. Within eight months, eight states had ratified. On June 21, 1788, New Hampshire became the ninth state to ratify, making the new Constitution legal. But neither New York nor Virginia had ratified, and both of these states were essential for the new government to exist at all, Virginia because of its importance and New York for its location.

Virginia finally ratified five days after New Hampshire, but not until the Antifederalists, led by Patrick Henry, Richard Henry Lee, and George Mason, extracted a concession for another national convention to consider amendments to protect individual liberties. The Federalists, led by Madison, agreed.

Meanwhile, New York watched carefully how the other states voted. The debate in that state had been particularly acrimonious. Most of the delegates were Antifederalist, but through the efforts of Hamilton, Jay, and Livingston, the opposition was won over, and New York ratified the Constitution by a margin of three votes.

Hamilton was particularly persuasive during the debates. At the outset, he conceived the idea of publishing a series of essays under the pseudonym "Publius" to persuade the public to approve the new Constitution. Eighty-five of these essays were published by three Federalists (Hamilton, Madison, and Jay) in the New York papers. Later, the essays were compiled into a book under the title *The Federalist*. As Garry Wills has noted, "The essays overwhelmed re-

sponse."[20] The essays, even today, articulate the best expo-
sition on the Constitution as seen by the founders.

Once the new government was formed in April 1789,
one of the first acts of the new congress was to keep the
Federalist promise to append to the Constitution a bill of
rights. James Madison led Congress to consider twelve
amendments, ten of which were approved on December 15,
1791. (See appendix 3.) These amendments, designated
today as the Bill of Rights, may correctly be considered part
of the original Constitution.

Why the Philadelphia Constitutional Convention Was So Extraordinary

The Constitutional Convention lasted from May 25 to
September 17, just over three and a half months. The
framers devised a document that established a federal government to protect the rights of U. S. citizens in their day;
this was a significant accomplishment in itself. But what is
really extraordinary is that the charter they created has
proved sufficiently practical and flexible to govern a nation
with a population of over 200 million two centuries later.

Significant is the fact that the founders of the republic
were not satisfied to live under monarchical rule (their
tradition for centuries), nor to exist as separate states with
governors over them (their tradition for a century), nor to
live under a federation (their tradition of less than a decade).
They forged a democratic republic with no parallel tradition
in history.

The Articles of Confederation demonstrated that to
write rules by law is not a guarantee that its provisions will
be enforced. Countries may draft constitutions with idealis-
tic provisions, but to make them work is quite another
matter.

There are at least four reasons why this new government
worked where others have not. First, the provisions of the
document were formed in what Washington called a "spirit
of accommodation."[21] The framers made concessions and
compromises that were in the best interests of the young

nation's survival. This accommodation was based on what they considered the public virtue—what was good for the whole. They put aside their jealousies and partisan concerns in the interest of a union. Second, the entire process depended on the direct or indirect consent of the people. The constitutional assemblage at Philadelphia was supported by the delegates of the sovereign states. Thus the Constitution was an emanation from the people. They sent the delegates, ordained the document, and established the government. The government that came into being in April 1789 was not a concession to them by a sovereign power; it was the creation of a sovereign people. Third, the people bound themselves to be governed by law and not by rulers, in the English tradition that recognized that the laws of God were superior to the laws of society and that all people had rights specific and inherent at birth. All judges, legislators, and officers were henceforth oath-bound ("so help me God") to "support the Constitution" as the supreme law of the land. Fourth, their efforts were undeniably inspired by God. When their work was completed, the Lord subsequently declared that the new Constitution was "justifiable" before Him and that He had "established the Constitution . . . by the hands of wise men" whom He had "raised up." (D&C 98:5; 101:80.) Thus a new government was established, foreseen and prophesied in the Book of Mormon, that made the United States of America "a land of liberty." (See 2 Nephi 10:10-14.)

The founders not only forged a document that governs our nation, but one that fulfilled Washington's hope that a standard would be raised to which the wise and honest would repair. That standard was raised. In tribute to the Constitution, President Joseph Fielding Smith said that it is "the greatest document . . . ever adopted by organized society for their government, outside of the kingdom of God."[22]

4

"For the Rights and Protection of All Flesh"

It was from America that the plain ideas that men
ought to mind their own business, and that the
nation is responsible to Heaven for the acts of
State—ideas long locked in the breasts of solitary
thinkers, and hidden among Latin folios,—burst
forth like a conqueror upon the world they were
destined to transform, under the title of the Rights
of Man.

Lord Acton

aving considered the background of the development of the Constitution, we shall now turn our attention to an explanation of the "just and holy principles" the Lord approved that were to protect the rights of "all flesh."
The chief complaint of the critics of the new Constitution was the lack of a bill of rights. To many, particularly the small farmers who had been the backbone of the revolution, the rights of the people was what the revolution represented. But the new Constitution only implied these rights. Only after the Federalists promised to make these rights specific and explicit did the key states ratify it; therefore, it is not improper to think of the first ten amendments (the Bill of Rights) as a part of the original Constitution.

Four vital questions that affect the rights of the people were answered by the formation of a constitutional republic. As we consider each one, we can better appreciate how a constitutional system of government was designed to protect and safeguard these rights.

1. *What is the basis of our right to life, liberty, and property?* The distinction between civil law and common law is fundamental to understanding the Constitution. President J. Reuben Clark, Jr., provided an explanation in a masterful treatise entitled "Let Us Not Sell Our Children into Slavery."[1] Briefly, his explanation is this: In a general sense, there are only two governmental systems in the world today. The European tradition recognized that the sovereign power was vested in the head of state (a monarchy or dictatorship) or a group of rulers (an oligarchy). Its basis is Roman or civil law and rests on the premise that rulers grant to the people the rights and powers the rulers think the people should have. All dictatorships have recognized this system. Regardless of how benevolent the dictators may be, the system denies that which belongs to all people *inalienably*—their right to life, liberty, and property. Furthermore, such a political philosophy causes the people to be subservient to the state or to human rulers, thereby violating the will of heaven that "it is not right that any man should be in bondage one to another." (D&C 101:79.)

The Founding Fathers deliberately rejected the European system of civil law because it had historically caused tyranny and subjugation and denied the people their rights. But, more important, they were indoctrinated in a different system of thought—the British system of common law, based on the principle that sovereignty rests with the people. This conception of law is illustrated by the opening clause in the Preamble to the Constitution: "*We the people of the United States* . . . do ordain and establish . . ."

In this statement, the people were declared to be sovereign, not a king, emperor, oligarchy, or state. All rights and powers not granted specifically to the government were retained to themselves. This, as President J. Reuben Clark, Jr., pointed out, was the difference between freedom and despotism.

To say that the people were recognized as being sovereign was not to contradict the biblical truth (accepted by the founders) that God is the source of all human rights—and is therefore supremely sovereign. The founders subscribed to the philosophy of *natural rights,* the doctrine that people have inherent rights to life, liberty, and property.

John Adams expressed it this way: "All men are born free and *independent,* and have certain natural, essential, and unalienable rights, among which may be reckoned the right of enjoying and defending their lives and liberties; that of acquiring, possessing, and protecting property; in fine, that of seeking and obtaining their safety and happiness."[2]

What is the basis of our rights to life, liberty, and property? The answer provided by the founders was that the rights are unalienable, meaning that the rights could neither be surrendered not transferred to another. All people receive these rights at birth. In 1833 the Lord revealed to Joseph Smith that the Constitution, which the Lord "suffered to be established," was to be "maintained for the rights and protection of all flesh." (D&C 101:77.)

2. *How should the power of government be limited?* In order to safeguard these inalienable rights, the founders provided three specific limitations of power in our written constitution.

A *first* way the power of government was limited is that the power was distributed to states and local governments. This is the concept of federalism.

One of the great fears, as shown by the debates at the Constitutional Convention, was that power would be concentrated in a centralized government. The founders solved that problem by deliberately devising two overlapping governments: one national (which united the states into a federal republic); the other, the states and local governments. These two levels of government were to exist simultaneously. Power was to be divided between each, and each would act as a check on the other.

Powers delegated to the federal government were to be "few and defined" and to be concerned with "war, peace, negotiation, and foreign commerce."[3] The Constitution specifically limits the powers that belong to the federal government by enumerating the things it could do, among which were raising and maintaining an armed force, raising taxes, forming treaties and alliances, conducting commerce with foreign nations, and coining money.

But the greater powers were to be retained by the states, the object being to keep the government close to the people. "The powers reserved to the several States will extend to all the objects which . . . concern the lives, liberties, and properties of the people, and the internal order, improvement, and prosperity of the State."[4]

Among powers granted to the states were these: presidential electors were to be chosen in a manner prescribed by the states; equal representation was given to each state in the Senate; senators originally were to be elected only by state legislators; amendments to the Constitution were possible only by large majorities—three-fourths of the state legislatures—or by the demands of the several states for a constitutional convention; members of the House of Representatives were chosen by districts within each state; and states retained control over most of the police force and court issues dealing with life, liberty, or property.

Furthermore, the tenth amendment of the Bill of Rights reserved to the states all powers not delegated to the federal government.

The purpose of the framers decentralizing power to the states and local government was to preserve maximum "home rule"—to keep the power closest to the people. This was recognized as the only way in which the principles of self-government could operate effectively and without coercion.

But there were also limitations on the states. States were prohibited under the Constitution from making treaties or alliances, coining money, issuing bills of credit, and making anything but gold and silver legal tender in payment of debts. Moreover, each state was to have a republican form of government, namely, a representative form of government created by a written constitution that specifically limited the government by dividing it into three separate branches—executive, legislative, and judicial.

Thus, the founders created, in Madison's phrase, "a compound republic," the advantages being that power is "divided between two distinct governments. . . . Hence, a double security arises to the rights of the people."[5] For, "if one encroaches on their rights, they will find a powerful protection in the other. Indeed, they will both be prevented from overpassing their constitutional limits, by a certain rivalship."[6]

Rivalship for power between the national and state governments was anticipated. And our two-hundred-year history has shown that when an inordinate amount of power shifts to one group, national unity and liberty becomes endangered. The Civil War, for example, was precipitated over the constitutional question of states having authority to secede from the Union. That crisis threatened the very existence of the republic.

A *second* way the power of government is limited is that the functions of government were separated into three branches: executive, legislative, and judicial. Almost all the framers of the Constitution perceived government to be a reflection of human nature, which they considered as having a disposition toward power and self-aggrandizement. Therefore, they incorporated into the Constitution the fundamental provision to check tyrannical power of the government by separating its functions into three distinct branches. This doctrine had been earlier espoused by Montesquieu and Locke, who believed that the way to limit government power was to divide its functions.

The functions of each branch were not to be delegated to other branches, nor to encroach on the others. Their functions were to be separate and independent yet interdependent. This blending of independence from each other, and dependence on each other, said J. Reuben Clark, Jr., "constitutes the marvelous genius of this unrivaled document. . . . It was here that the divine inspiration came. It was truly a miracle."[7]

The independence of each branch may best be appreciated as we consider provisions within the Constitution that protect one branch from the other. Thus, the president of the United States protects himself by a veto power and promises of patronage. The Congress protects itself by setting its own pay, making its own rules, and judging its own members. The Supreme Court has a lifetime tenure and may not have salaries reduced during that tenure.

In two centuries of application, this remarkable principle—separation of powers—has demonstrated that one branch may prove to be a check on the human tendency to usurp more power to its own branch. The term *Watergate* has become almost synonymous with the abuse of power, but we should also remember that two branches of government—the legislative and the judicial—successfully and cooperatively checked such an abuse of power by the executive branch.

A *third* way the power of government is limited is that checks and balances were incorporated into the Constitution. In order to maintain the independence of each branch, the founders provided that steps could be taken to check usurpation by another branch to protect its own independence (balance). The way the framers incorporated these checks and balances throughout the Constitution was ingenious.

Congress checks the president by refusing to appropriate money to the executive branch. By majority vote, it may reject presidential appointments and administrative agencies. The Senate can reject any treaties made by the president, since a two-thirds vote of the Senate is required to ratify treaties. The president may take action toward war, but only Congress can declare it. The House of Representatives can impeach a president (charge him with malfeasance of office), but only the Senate, who approves lifetime appointments, can try those officers who are charged with impeachable offenses.

Congress checks the judicial department by its power to abolish lower courts, and it may limit the courts' appellate jurisdiction because the jurisdiction is subject to "such exceptions, and under such regulations as the Congress shall make." Congress can also impeach federal judges.

The president can veto any legislation by the Congress, although his veto can be overridden by a two-thirds vote of both houses. The president can, with the approval of the Senate, influence the direction of the court by his power to appoint federal judges.

The Supreme Court can check the other two branches by declaring legislation by Congress or acts by the president unconstitutional.

Each branch of the government was also made subject to different political pressures. The president was to be chosen by electors, senators by state legislatures, representatives by the people, and the Supreme Court by the president with the consent of the Senate.

The use of checks and balances was, as John Adams said, "to create delays and multiply diversities of interests, by which the tendency on a sudden to violate them may be counteracted."[8]

3. *How are minority rights protected?* Recognizing that the majority is omnipotent in a democracy, the founders deliberately devised a constitutional republic described by Jefferson as "action by the citizens in person, in affairs within their reach and competence, and in all others by representatives."[9] The republic they established was one where the people adopted a written constitution that defined how their views would be represented. Universal suffrage was regarded as a dangerous experiment, particularly if the masses were neither intelligent nor virtuous.

The original Constitution provided for both direct representation (representatives elected directly by the people) and indirect representation (officers of government elected by legislative bodies who were elected by the people). These two forms of representation were deliberately devised by the framers to protect minority rights.

As a "concession to the democratic principle," to use Winston Churchill's phrase, the House of Representatives was chosen directly by the people. This body of the national legislature was directly responsible to the majority of the electorate. To make certain they would be responsive to the people, their term of office was limited to only two years.

The Senate, however, was elected by the state legislatures to a six-year term of office. Not being elected directly
by the people, this body would not be so susceptible to
exchanging political favors for votes and could therefore
prevent precipitous or impulsive legislation by the lower
House. In this way, a restraining check was placed on the
House of Representatives, who would be most directly
influenced by the will and demands of the majority. As a
further protection, no legislation or bill could pass without
the majority approval of both the House and the Senate.
Thus the system protected the interests of the minority.[10]

The original system, of course, was altered by the Seventeenth Amendment, so that today both House and Senate
are elected by direct popular vote. Also, there are current
efforts to further democratize this republican system of
government by eliminating the electoral college, which
would further rescind the feature of indirect representation
for the executive. The effect of this action may well turn the
government to the will of the majority, leaving minority and
individual rights further unguarded and unprotected. Surely
today we are more vulnerable as a society to "spectacles of
turbulence and contention," as Madison warned,[11] and this
departure in philosophy from the original intent of the
founders has made our legislative bodies, as the late Sir
Henry Sumner Maine said, "the mere reflection of the
average opinion of the multitude."[12]

4. *How are individual rights protected?* Fundamental
to the philosophy of the founders was their belief that no
person could be deprived of certain rights—life, liberty, and
property. When the Lord said that the Constitution of the
United States was to "be maintained for the *rights* and protection of all flesh," He further explained that such protection was essential so that we could fully exercise the moral
agency that has been accorded to us, "that every man may
be accountable for his own sins in the day of judgment."
(D&C 101:77-78; italics added.) Protection of individual
rights was expressly stated in the Bill of Rights. Before the

Bill of Rights was added, the Constitution itself guaranteed certain protections to one's liberty. These four provisions were:

1. The right to a trial by jury, of all violations of federal law, in the state where the crime is committed.

2. The right to habeas corpus. This was an old common-law writ that commands the release of a person who is being illegally detained. A writ of habeas corpus is an order from a judge directing that a person held in custody · be brought before the court to determine whether he or she is being held lawfully. If the person is being held unlawfully, the court will order his or her release.

3. The Constitution forbade Congress to pass ex post facto laws. This simply means that a person may not be punished for violating a law if the law had not been passed when the action occurred.

4. Congress is forbidden to pass a bill of attainder. These bills were fairly common in early English history and permitted punishment of the individual without a trial. Under the Constitution, only a court may punish someone for violating a law; a legislative body may not.

But as a further protection to the basic rights, the first ten amendments were added. The founders recognized that the people already had these rights and immunities before the Constitution came into existence, but the Bill of Rights was written to secure these liberties against government oppression.

These are the basic provisions of the first ten amendments:

1. The First Amendment protects the individual's right to freedom of religion, freedom of speech, freedom of the press, and freedom to assemble and to petition the government for a redress of grievances.[13] Significant to Latter-day Saints is the first clause of this amendment: "Congress shall make no law respecting an establishment of religion or prohibiting the free exercise thereof." Without freedom of religion, there could be no promulgation of the gospel, and

the plan of God would be thwarted because people would be unable to exercise their agency to choose. Without such freedom they could not be accountable for their sins.

2. The Second Amendment does not confer the right to bear arms; it prevents congress from infringing on that right.

3. The Third Amendment protects an individual's right against military intrusion into his or her home without consent.

4. The Fourth Amendment protects the individual's right against unreasonable search and seizure. Before officers of law can search someone's property, they must show a warrant that evidences good reason to suppose the person is guilty of wrongdoing.

5. The Fifth Amendment protects the individual's right against double jeopardy, meaning that one cannot be tried twice for the same offense; the right against self-incrimination; the right to "due process of law" (presumption of innocence till proven guilty); and the right against having property taken without just compensation.

6. The Sixth Amendment protects the individual's right to a trial by jury, to a speedy and public trial, to be informed of charges against him or her, to be confronted by witnesses, and to have legal counsel.

7. The Seventh Amendment protects the individual's right to a trial by jury in common-law cases. This refers only to federal courts, and only to cases arising out of common law.

8. The Eighth Amendment protects one's right against excessive bail, fines, and cruel and unusual punishment. This right is also protected by the fourteenth amendment, which prevents states from depriving any person of life, liberty, or property without due process of law.

9. The Ninth Amendment protects other rights that may not have been mentioned in the Constitution.

10. The Tenth Amendment makes clear that the federal government has only the powers that have been delegated to it. All other powers not so delegated are reserved to the people.

All people possess at birth the rights to life, liberty, and property! Therefore, a governmental system was devised, based on "just and holy principles," to protect those rights. It was for this purpose that the Lord inspired the creation of the Constitution and then sanctioned the work performed by its framers. (See D&C 101:77-80; 98:6.)

The critical feature of the Constitution is not in the words, phrases, clauses, or provisions of the document itself, but rather in the "vigilant and manly spirit which actuates the people of America—a spirit which nourishes freedom, and in return is nourished by it."[14] Therefore to preserve the advantages of liberty—and to maintain the spirit of the Constitution, there must be "a frequent recurrence to the fundamental principles of the constitution, and a constant adherence to those of piety, justice, moderation, temperance, industry and frugality."[15]

Three immutable principles need constant affirmation if the spirit of the Constitution, not just the letter of the law, is to be kept alive and the rights of the people preserved.

The first fundamental is that all people are created by God and possess at birth inherent rights pertaining to life, liberty, and property. This philosophy is rooted in the Fatherhood of God and the brotherhood of humanity and naturally fosters regard and respect toward one's fellows. When this belief is upheld, honesty, integrity, and respect for the property and possessions and person of others is demonstrated in personal relationships. When this belief does not prevail, as it does not among many societies and governments, the social consequences are apparent. People are seen as creatures of the government, and the state as the benefactor of their rights. President Ezra Taft Benson has profoundly written about the implications of this philosophy:

> When human law is regarded as the only source of men's rights, any leader may act capriciously toward his fellow beings. He may deny privileges such as free expression and require even the forfeiture of life. The 20th century has witnessed monstrously evil consequences

justified with euphemisms such as *resettlement, pogroms, reeducation,* until a *final solution* was decreed.

Likewise, consequences of agnosticism are enormous, particularly when this value is fostered by the state. How does a nation take a stand against the moral evils of totalitarianism if leaders do not recognize a source of law higher than man's? On what grounds may we morally object? The inhumanity of man toward his fellow man is the result of a forgotten relationship to God. When such a value is obscured, the relationship toward one's fellow beings also becomes ambivalent![16]

A second fundamental is that all people, as creations of God, are to act and not to be acted upon. By the use of their agency, they are accountable for their actions. People should have the freedom to determine their own fate and destiny, even if wrong. This includes the freedom to reason, speak, make economic and spiritual decisions, and provide for their own and their family's welfare without the dictates of government. This freedom unleashes their initiative, inventiveness, and creative potential. Personal and national prosperity soon follow. But when these rights are denied expression, people become spiritually enslaved, human progress is inhibited, and misery follows.

A third fundamental is that religious liberty is inextricably bound to political and economic freedoms. The four great freedoms, freedom of speech, freedom of assembly, freedom of the press, and freedom of religion, are interrelated and cannot be treated separately. As Samuel Adams noted, they rise and fall together. The Reverend John Witherspoon, president of Princeton and signer of the Declaration of Independence, similarly stated, "There is not a single instance in history in which civil liberty was lost, and religious liberty preserved entire. If we yield up our temporal property, we at the same time deliver the conscience into bondage."[17]

The establishment of the American republic, based on a written constitution, created a unique philosophy that has permeated the free world. It has given the world an example of prosperity never before witnessed in its history. It has kindled a desire on the part of millions of immigrants to come to this country for opportunity and freedom. It has provided an example of the sanctity of human rights, property ownership, and respect for law, justice, and freedom. That is why the United States Constitution is emulated by all who love liberty. And that is why it is the charter of liberty for all people.

"That Every Man Might Be Accountable"

I the Lord will hold the courts, with the officers of
government, and the nation responsible for their
acts towards the inhabitants of Zion.
Revelation to President
Wilford Woodruff
Sunday, November 24, 1889

ell known among the Latter-day Saints is the fact that the Lord gave sanction to the Constitution of the United States, but not well understood is the historic context out of which the revelations that pertain to the Constitution of the United States were given. Nor is it commonly understood why the Constitution is regarded in Latter-day Saint theology as essential in furthering the kingdom of God on this earth.

In the design of heaven, it was not sufficient that the colonies just be free and separate from England. This was to be a united republic, an ensign of liberty to all other nations. It was also to provide a cradle of freedom for an infant Church whose mission it is to establish Zion. God foreordained that from the shores of America, hosts of emissaries would bring the gospel of the restoration to all people "for the law shall go forth of Zion." (Micah 4:2.)

Prophets of God, past and present, foresaw the destiny of America and wrote of its glory. The Prophet Joseph Smith declared that America, both the northern and southern continents, comprise the land of Zion.[1] At a spot central to the United States of America, the Lord designated a place for a

future city to be called "the New Jerusalem, a land of peace,
a city of refuge, a place of safety for the saints of the Most
High God." (D&C 45:66-67.) It is an Article of Faith to Latter-
day Saints that Jesus Christ shall eventually come in His
glory to a holy sanctuary in that city.

Before Christ's glorious appearance, righteous men and
women will gather from the various portions of the earth to
establish a city of holiness to their God, crowned with a
temple to the Most High. This will be done by members of
the true church who have covenanted with God to forsake
their sins and to become sanctified before Him. They will
bear His priesthood, claim His name, perform ordinances in
His name, and promulgate His gospel to all people and
nations. In contrast to the greedy, selfish, and materialistic
focus of the culture about them, this group of Saints will be
unified in purpose, righteous in action, purified in motive,
and unselfish in the care of the poor and needy among
them. To imagine a society of people motivated by charity,
concern, and cooperation rather than greed is to envision
Christianity in its ideal state.

The focus of The Church of Jesus Christ of Latter-day
Saints upon this noble goal from its beginning is not the
pursuit of a utopian scheme. It is a hope that future Saints
may attain to the same measure of goodness achieved by the
society of the prophet Enoch when God approvingly called
them Zion because of their righteousness (see Moses 7:18); it
is compliance with the law of God to the Church in this dispensation to "bring forth and establish the cause of Zion"
(D&C 6:6); it is faith in the word of the Lord concerning His
promise that Zion will be built on the American continent
(Article of Faith 10). But before this vision could be realized,
there had to exist a nation where freedom of religion could
be enjoyed in order that the Church of Christ would be able
to declare its message and carry out its divine mission to
establish Zion.

Between the implementation of the Constitution in 1789
and the time in which the priesthood of God was returned
to the earth in 1829 was an interval of four decades. In that

interval, two events took place that, in retrospect, served the purposes of God in laying the foundation of Zion in the American continent.

First was the declaration of the Monroe Doctrine—a unilateral policy of the United States government that provided protection for both North and South America from European interference.

Three administrations of U. S. presidents (Washington, Adams, and Jefferson) wisely and successfully followed a foreign policy of "peace, commerce, and honest friendship with all nations, entangling alliances with none."[2]

During the administration of James Madison, the United States became involved in another war of independence with Britain, the first declared by Congress under the new Constitution. Though the United States lost most of the land battles, the war established the country as an industrial nation and a modest sea power; but more important, the war was its last controversy with Great Britain. Thereafter, America and Great Britain fought side by side as allies.

By 1822, many countries in South America had fought wars of revolution to free themselves from Spanish and Portuguese rule. In establishing independence, many of these countries established constitutions based on the Constitution of the United States, so the United States felt sympathetic to their efforts toward independence. But Russia, Austria, and Prussia urged France to help Spain and Portugal restore their monarchical governments in the Americas. Russia, meanwhile, was laying claim to western Canada. This provoked the Monroe administration to issue the famous Monroe Doctrine, which warned these European nations that any efforts toward further colonization would be viewed as a hostile act by the United States. The proclamation had a deterring effect on further colonization attempts, but its real effectiveness was attributable to the sea power of America's new ally, Great Britain.

The Monroe Doctrine established the United States as a recognized international power that was able to safeguard its own borders and prevent incursion by European countries into the Latin American countries. In a prophetic sense, the land of Zion was protected from European domination.

A second significant event took place under the administration of President Thomas Jefferson with the Louisiana Purchase of 1803. This not only afforded western expansion, but it also brought into the United States the territory that would eventually be the centerplace of Zion.

Thus in those four decades (1789-1829), the United States was able to protect the hemisphere from foreign encroachment and had added Florida and the Louisiana territory to its borders. Internally the country was strengthened by feelings of nationalism. Manufacturing and inventions made the new nation a part of the Industrial Revolution. The country was coming of age, enabling it to provide a cradle of freedom for the birthplace of the Church of Jesus Christ.

The new Church, founded in 1830 in the state of New York, was established by revelation on the premise that the ancient church of Christ had been lost through apostasy. By the end of 1830, the Lord commanded the Church to move to Ohio. Kirtland became headquarters for the Church, and for a period of seven years revelations were received by the Prophet Joseph Smith that established and expanded the government of God on earth and laid a foundation for the society of Zion. But it was not until the Prophet brought a portion of the Church's membership into western Missouri that the significance of that place and the Lord's purposes were revealed.

To a number of elders who had come from Kirtland, Ohio, to Missouri with the Prophet Joseph Smith, the Lord revealed that "Missouri . . . is the land which I have appointed and consecrated for the gathering of the saints. Wherefore, this is the land of promise, *and the place for the city of Zion.* . . . Behold, the place which is now called Independence is the center place; and a spot for the temple is lying westward. (D&C 57:13; italics added.)

On August 1, 1831, the Lord revealed to the Saints in Missouri that He had brought them here that they "might be

honored in *laying the foundation,* and in bearing record of
the land upon which the Zion of God shall stand." (D&C
58:7; italics added.) Zion was promised to be a condition of
glory, but it would not be brought about until after "much
tribulation." (See D&C 58:3-5.) That tribulation for the early
settlers in Missouri was not long waiting.

Missouri, a slave state, had applied for statehood in
1818. This precipitated a national controversy that centered
not on the morality of slavery, but on the objection of the
Northern States that by admitting new slave states, they
would receive a disproportionate representation in Congress, since 60 percent of the slaves were counted to determine the size of the states' delegations in the House of
Representatives. In 1819, the Union had eleven free states
and eleven slave states. Northerners saw Missouri's inclusion
into the Union as an attempt to increase the voting power of
the South.[3] By the famous Missouri Compromise, Missouri
was permitted to enter the Union as a slave state[4] and Maine
as a free state, thus keeping the balance between slave and
free states equal.

When Church members settled in Jackson County, there
was a natural ideological conflict between them and the
Missouri settlers. The old settlers were from the South and
upheld slavery. They resented the Mormons, most of whom
were from the eastern states, and feared that they would
gain political control of the state. The problem was further
exacerbated by the fact that some Church members un-
wisely let it be known that Missouri was to be the place of
their inheritance and the city of Zion. Great resentment by
other non-Mormon citizens was generated when the Church
members purchased land in western Missouri. In 1833 the
hostility came to a head.

On July 20, 1833, a group of Missourians presented to
the elders of the Church a list of "demands" that no Mormons would thereafter settle in Jackson County and that
those already there would give a "definite pledge of their
intention within a reasonable time to remove out of the
county." Also, the Church was to refrain from publishing

their newspaper, the *Evening and Morning Star.* These demands, of course, required a forfeiture of property rights, religious freedom, and freedom of the press, clearly a violation of the Constitution of the United States. When presented to local Church elders, the demands were refused. The local non-Mormon citizens responded by destroying the press of the *Star* and by tarring and feathering the editor and his assistant.

Three days later, a mob of about five hundred men threatened the scourging and death of every Latter-day Saint man, woman, and child if they would not leave Jackson County. Presented with this prospect, the elders of the Church were forced to agree to these terms: By January 1, 1834, the leading elders, along with their families, were to leave, in addition to one-half of the Church members; the other half was to leave by April 1. If the terms were met, the Missourians promised to refrain from violence. That promise was not honored, and the depredations and persecution that followed became a context for important revelations to the Saints relative to upholding constitutional government.

Kirtland, Ohio, the headquarters of the Church, was about eight hundred miles from Independence, Missouri. Communication had not come to the First Presidency concerning the extent of the persecution in Missouri, so Oliver Cowdery was sent to advise them. Two weeks before Oliver Cowdery arrived at Kirtland, the Lord told Joseph Smith, "It is my will that my people should observe to do all things whatsoever I command them. And that law of the land which is constitutional, supporting that principle of freedom in maintaining rights and privileges, belongs to all mankind, and is justifiable before me. . . .

"Therefore, I, the Lord, justify you, and your brethren of my church, in befriending that which is the constitutional law of the land; and as pertaining to law of man, whatsoever is more or less than this, cometh of evil. I, the Lord God, make you free, therefore ye are free indeed; and the law also maketh you free. Nevertheless, when the wicked rule the people mourn. Wherefore, honest men and wise men should be sought for diligently; and good and wise men ye should observe to uphold; otherwise whatsoever is less than these cometh of evil." (D&C 98:4-10.)

The Church was commanded to renounce war and proclaim peace, an extraordinary request for forbearance under their circumstances. The Saints were also told under what circumstances they could retaliate against their enemies. They were given the "law of Nephi," namely, if their enemy struck them, they were commanded to forgive at least three times, after which the Lord would deliver their enemy into their hands. (D&C 98:23-32.) They were told that the only conditions by which they would be justified in going to war was that their enemies refused repeated peace offers, and only if the Lord commanded. (D&C 98:32-38.) If their enemies repented, they were to forgive. (D&C 98:39-43.) Seek peace, forbear, forgive your enemies—trying counsel under circumstances where one's life, liberty, and property are threatened!

When the First Presidency learned more fully of the sufferings of the Saints in Missouri, they sent word for the Saints to seek redress from the governor. The Missouri Saints did so. After receiving the petition of grievances, Governor Dunklin replied that they should take their grievances to court. Even though the advice was followed, it was futile because the local judges, clerks, and constable were in conspiracy with the lieutenant governor of the state, Lilburn Boggs, to dispossess the Mormons of their property. In contravention of their own agreement not to resort to violence, the local citizens of Jackson County took the law into their own hands and proclaimed open war against the local Church members. Repeated attacks were made on Mormon communities, and much property was destroyed. At the direction of Boggs, the state militia was called out to suppress the attacks, but within the ranks of the militia were those who greatly opposed the Mormons. The militia demanded that the Saints surrender their arms. They agreed to do so on the condition that the mob also disarm. When

Boggs gave his word to that agreement, the elders of the Church complied, but arms were never taken from the mob. With the members of the Church disarmed, the mob commenced a murderous attack against them. They destroyed 203 homes and forced into exile twelve hundred members of the Church.

The Prophet's journal history recounts some of the nightmarish scenes of depredation:

> Thursday night, the 31st of October, gave the Saints in Zion abundant proof that no pledge on the part of their enemies, written or verbal, was longer to be regarded; for on that night, between forty and fifty persons in number, many of whom were armed with guns, proceeded against a branch of the Church, west of the Big Blue, and unroofed and partly demolished ten dwelling houses; and amid the shrieks and screams of the women and children, whipped and beat in a savage and brutal manner, several of the men: while their horrid threats frightened women and children into the wilderness. Such of the men as could escape fled for their lives; for very few of them had arms, neither were they organized; and they were threatened with death if they made any resistance; such therefore as could not escape by flight, received a pelting with stones and a beating with guns and whips. On Friday, the first of November, women and children sallied forth from their gloomy retreats, to contemplate with heartrending anguish the ravages of a ruthless mob, in the lacerated and bruised bodies of their husbands, and in the destruction of their houses, and their furniture. Houseless and unprotected by the arm of the civil law in Jackson county, the dreary month of November staring them in the face and loudly proclaiming an inclement season at hand; the continual threats of the mob that they would drive every "Mormon" from the county; and the inability of many to move, because of their poverty, caused an anguish of heart indescribable.
>
> On Friday night, the 1st of November, a party of the mob proceeded to attack a branch of the Church settled on the prairie, about twelve or fourteen miles from the town of Independence. . . .

The same night, (Friday), another party in Independence commenced stoning houses, breaking down doors
and windows and destroying furniture. . . .

Thursday, November 7th, the shores of the Missouri
river began to be lined on both sides of the ferry, with
men, women and children; goods, wagons, boxes, chests,
and provisions; while the ferrymen were busily employed
in crossing them over. When night again closed upon the
Saints, the wilderness had much the appearance of a camp
meeting. Hundreds of people were seen in every direction; some in tents, and some in the open air, around their
fires, while the rain descended in torrents. Husbands were
inquiring for their wives, and women for their husbands;
parents for children, and children for parents. Some had
the good fortune to escape with their families, household
goods, and some provisions; while others knew not the
fate of their friends, and had lost all their effects. The
scene was indescribable, and would have melted the
hearts of any people upon earth, except the blind oppres-
sor, and the prejudiced and ignorant bigot. . . .

The Saints who fled from Jackson county, took refuge
in the neighboring counties, chiefly in Clay county, the
inhabitants of which received them with some degree of
kindness. Those who fled to the county of Van Buren
were again driven, and compelled to flee, and these who
fled to Lafayette county, were soon expelled, or the most
of them, and had to move wherever they could find protection.[5]

Many died in that ordeal, but the majority found refuge
in neighboring counties. Thus their residence in a county
and land regarded as sacred to them was denied; the
property they had lawfully purchased was forfeited. Reflect-
ing on the terrible injustice to the Saints, the Prophet
lamented: "The heart sickens at the recital. . . . More than
once, those people, in this boasted land of liberty, were
brought into jeopardy, and threatened with expulsion or
death, because they desired to worship God according to
the revelations of heaven, the constitution of their country,
and the dictates of their own consciences. Oh, liberty, how
art thou fallen!"[6]

When the Prophet received word about the forcible expulsion of the Saints from Jackson County, he wrote the
Saints a letter of great empathy and love, reminding them
what the Lord had said earlier: "After *much* tribulation come
the blessings." (D&C 58:4; italics added.) He then confided
that the Lord had not answered him regarding two questions: (1) "Why God has suffered so great a calamity to come
upon Zion, and what the great moving cause of this great
affliction is"; and (2) "By what means He will return her
back to her inheritance, with songs of everlasting joy upon
her head."[7] The answers came six days later—December 16,
1834—at Kirtland, Ohio.

Two reasons were given for the affliction and persecution of the Missouri Saints. First, they needed to be chastened and tried, "even as Abraham," and, second, the Lord
had permitted the sufferings to come to them in consequence of their transgressions, which were "jarrings, and
contentions, and envyings, and strifes, and lustful and
covetous desires." (D&C 101:2, 4, 6.) The Saints had been
"slow to hearken to the voice of the Lord their God;" therefore, he was slow to hear their petitions. Nevertheless, the
Lord promised, "I will own them, and they shall be mine in
that day when I shall come to make up my jewels. . . . I will
not utterly cast them off." (D&C 101:3, 7, 9.) Most
significantly, the Lord promised, "Zion shall not be moved
out of her place, notwithstanding her children are
scattered." (D&C 101:17.) In due time, the pure in heart
would return and build up "the waste places of Zion." (D&C
101:18.) The Saints were commanded to continue to seek
redress from judges, governors, and presidents; and if the
president would not heed them, the Lord would "vex the
nation." For, he said, "It is my will that they should
continue to importune for redress, and redemption, by the
hands of those who are placed as rulers and are in authority
over you." (D&C 101:76.) The reason they were to use
constitutional procedures rather than retaliation was given
as follows: "According to the laws and constitution of the
people, which I have suffered to be established, and should

be maintained for the rights and protection of all flesh, according to just and holy principles; that every man may act in doctrine and principle pertaining to futurity, according to the moral agency which I have given unto him, *that every man may be accountable for his own sins in the day of judgment.*" (D&C 101:77-78; italics added.)

The main body of the Saints found temporary refuge in Clay County. But when outbreaks of violence threatened them there, they were requested to leave. They had been driven from New York to Ohio, to Jackson County to Clay County; now they were forced to move again.

The Missouri legislature created Caldwell County in 1836 as a place where the Mormons could settle. The members of the Church purchased lands and once again began to build a community. They also settled in two other counties, Daviess and Carroll.

Their brief peace and respite in northern Missouri, however, lasted less than two years. Concerned that the Mormons might become a dominant political majority in the state, their old enemies aroused suspicion and jealousy. A small community political election became the tinder that eventually fueled dormant flames of hostility toward the Mormons and resulted in an "ultimate solution"—an extermination order by the governor—and the expulsion of the Mormons from the state of Missouri.

August 6, 1838, was election day in Gallatin, Daviess County. William Peniston, an anti-Mormon candidate for the legislature, stirred up the voters with the charge that if the Mormons were allowed to vote, the other settlers would lose their rights. When the Mormons went to vote, they were prevented from doing so. A fight ensued, and even though a small group of Mormon voters (about twelve) were badly outnumbered, they held their ground. The Prophet later commended them for so vigorously contending for their constitutional rights and religious freedom.[8]

When the Prophet Joseph Smith came to Gallatin to investigate the matter, the local justice of the peace certified that he would uphold the Constitution of the United States and not support the mob. But two days later he, along with Peniston and other anti-Mormons, signed an affidavit that 500 armed Mormons had descended on the town of Gallatin for the purpose of driving out the old settlers. Such a claim, of course, was a blatant falsehood.

Lilburn Boggs, an avowed enemy of the Mormons, was now governor of the state. When he received false reports that the Mormons were in a state of insurrection and were preparing for war against the old settlers, he ordered out the militia from each of the northern counties—a force of about twenty-eight hundred men. In their ranks were many bitter enemies of the Church. Armed with the sanction of the highest authority in the state, they could now legally carry out their persecutions on the Mormons.

The community of DeWitt, in Carroll County, was laid under seige. Even though his own militia officers informed Governor Boggs that actions of the Saints were defensive and that there was nothing to fear from the Mormons, he responded, "The quarrel [is] between the Mormons and the mob," and he said that they could fight it out.[9] Appeals were even made on behalf of the Mormons by nonmembers, but Boggs ignored them. Finally, the Saints were compelled to leave DeWitt.

In Caldwell County, the militia had captured three Mormon settlers. David W. Patten, a Church apostle, led a small company against the militia at Crooked River to rescue the prisoners. A battle ensued, and Patten and Gideon Carter were killed. Another died later from wounds. The militia reported to the governor and falsely accused the Mormons of promoting a civil war. On October 27, 1838, an infamous day in the history of Missouri, the state's governor issued an "Order of Extermination." "The Mormons," he wrote, "must be treated as enemies and *must be exterminated* or driven from the state, if necessary for the public good."[10]

Three days later a mob militia carried out the brutal massacre at Haun's Mill, where seventeen defenseless people were shot and killed.

The day following, the militia attacked Far West, plundered the town, destroyed the property, whipped the men, and raped the women, some of whom died. The Prophet and others were arrested, and the militia held a court martial. Without legal defense, or without making an appearance before the court, the prisoners were sentenced to death by firing squad. General Alexander Doniphan was ordered to carry out the execution but defied the orders of his superiors on the basis that it was "cold-blooded murder." His heroic action prevented their execution. Subsequently, Joseph Smith and his companions were incarcerated at the Richmond, Missouri, prison to await trial. After a sham trial, they were imprisoned in the jail at Liberty, Missouri, for five months under the most barbaric conditions. Despite these illegalities, the Prophet magnanimously wrote of the Constitution:

> We say, that the Constitution of the United States is a glorious standard; it is founded in the wisdom of God. It is a heavenly banner; it is to all those who are privileged with the sweets of its liberty, like the cooling shades and refreshing waters of a great rock in a thirsty and weary land. It is like a great tree under whose branches men from every clime can be shielded from the burning rays of the sun.
>
> We . . . are deprived of the protection of its glorious principles, by the cruelty of the cruel, by those who only look for the time being, for pasturage like the beasts of the field, only to fill themselves; and forget that the "Mormons," as well as the Presbyterians, and those of every other class and description, have equal rights to partake of the fruits of the great tree of our national liberty. But not withstanding we see what we see, and feel what we feel, and know what we know, yet that fruit is no less precious and delicious to our taste; we cannot be weaned from the milk, neither can we be driven from the breast; neither will we deny our religion because of the hand of oppression; but we will hold on until death.
>
> We say that God is true; that the Constitution of the United States is true.[11]

When the Saints were forced to leave Jackson County in

1833, they numbered about twelve hundred. All their property was confiscated. When they departed Clay County, they also left valuable property. Now, forced to leave the state, they numbered between twelve and fifteen thousand, and the property left behind was estimated at a value of over two million dollars.[12] And what price does one place on the loss of innocent lives—men, women, and children—whose "crime" was their religious beliefs?

The Saints eventually sought financial compensation from the Missouri legislature. Without an investigation, but to salve their consciences, a meager sum of $2,000 was appropriated for the "citizens" of Caldwell County, most of which never reached the Saints.

Obeying the Lord's command that "if the governor heed them not, let them importune at the feet of the president," the Prophet Joseph Smith went to Washington, D.C., in 1839 and on two occasions visited the president of the United States, Martin Van Buren, to detail their persecutions and grievances. This was done after the Church leaders had appealed to the governor of the state of Missouri and to the legislature of the state, all to no avail. The reason for the appeal was to bring to the attention of the people of the United States the inhumane treatment given to fellow citizens of the nation. In the appeal, the Prophet Joseph Smith said:

> I ask the citizens of this Republic whether such a state of things is to be suffered to pass unnoticed, and the hearts of widows, orphans, and patriots to be broken, and their wrongs left without redress? No! I invoke the genius of our Constitution. I appeal to the patriotism of Americans to stop this unlawful and unholy procedure; and pray that God may defend this nation from the dreadful effects of such outrages.
>
> Is there no virtue in the body politic? Will not the people rise up in their majesty, and with that promptitude and zeal which are so characteristic of them, discountenance such proceedings, by bringing the offenders to that punishment which they so richly deserve, and save the nation from that disgrace and ultimate ruin, which otherwise must inevitably fall upon it?[13]

In his second interview with President Van Buren, the Prophet reported that the president listened with great reluctance and then replied, "Gentlemen, your cause is just, but I can do nothing for you. If I take up for you I shall lose the vote of Missouri."[14] This reaction from the president of the United States provoked the Prophet to write: "[Van Buren's] whole course went to show that he was an office-seeker, that self-aggrandizement was his ruling passion, and that justice and righteousness were no part of his composition. I found him such a man as I could not conscientiously support at the head of our noble Republic."[15]

A further appeal was made to the Congress of the United States, but after a consideration of the charges, a congressional committee concluded that the "petitioners" (the members of the Church) "must seek relief in the courts of judicature of the state of Missouri."[16]

In spite of the fact that the Prophet was unable to obtain any legal satisfaction for the Saints by seeking redress from the courts of law, or from the nation's highest leaders, he again affirmed his loyalty to the Constitution but noted one defect:

> I am the greatest advocate of the Constitution of the United States there is on the earth. In my feelings I am always ready to die for the protection of the weak and oppressed in their just rights. The only fault I find with the Constitution is, it is not broad enough to cover the whole ground.
>
> Although it provides that all men shall enjoy religious freedom, yet it does not provide the manner by which that freedom can be preserved, nor for the punishment of Government officers who refuse to protect the people in their religious rights, or punish those mobs, states, or communities who interfere with the rights of the people on account of their religion. Its sentiments are good, but it provides no means of enforcing them. It has but this one fault. Under its provision, a man or a people who are able to protect themselves can get along well enough; but those who have the misfortune to be weak or unpopular are left to the merciless rage of popular fury.
>
> The Constitution should contain a provision that

every officer of the Government who should neglect or refuse to extend the protection guaranteed in the Constitution should be subject to capital punishment; and then the president of the United States would not say, *"Your cause is just, but I can do nothing for you,"* a governor issue exterminating orders, or judges say, "The men ought to have the protection of law, but it won't please the mob; the men must die, anyhow, to satisfy the clamor of the rabble; they must be hung, or Missouri be damned to all eternity." Executive writs could be issued when they ought to be, and not be made instruments of cruelty to oppress the innocent, and persecute men whose religion is unpopular.[17]

In the midst of the Missouri persecutions, the Saints were accused of disloyalty to the government, sedition, and rebellion. They had every reason to feel that their government, under the Constitution, had failed them. Yet, in spite of the injustices that came to them, they issued a declaration of belief that was included with the first edition of the Doctrine and Covenants, now designated as section 134. In the context of their deprived rights and loss of property in Missouri, the document constitutes a remarkable statement in support of government, law and order, and religious freedom:

We believe that governments were instituted of God for the benefit of man;[18] and that he holds men accountable for their acts in relation to them, both in making laws and administering them, for the good and safety of society.

We believe that no government can exist in peace, except such laws are framed and held inviolate as will secure to each individual the free exercise of conscience, the right and control of property, and the protection of life.

We believe that all governments necessarily require civil officers and magistrates to enforce the laws of the same; and that such as will administer the law in equity and justice should be sought for and upheld by the voice of the people if a republic, or the will of the sovereign.

We believe that religion is instituted of God; and that men are amenable to him, and to him only, for the exercise of it, unless their religious opinions prompt them to infringe upon the rights and liberties of others; but we do not believe that human law has a right to interfere in prescribing rules of worship to bind the consciences of men, nor dictate forms for public or private devotion; that the civil magistrate should restrain crime, but never control conscience; should punish guilt, but never suppress the freedom of the soul.

We believe that all men are bound to sustain and uphold the respective governments in which they reside, while protected in their inherent and inalienable rights by the laws of such governments; and that sedition and rebellion are unbecoming every citizen thus protected, and should be punished accordingly; and that all governments have a right to enact such laws as in their own judgments are best calculated to secure the public interest; at the same time, however, holding sacred the freedom of conscience.[19]

We believe that every man should be honored in his station, rulers and magistrates as such, being placed for the protection of the innocent and the punishment of the guilty; and that to the laws all men show respect and deference, as without them peace and harmony would be supplanted by anarchy and terror; human laws being instituted for the express purpose of regulating our interests as individuals and nations, between man and man; and divine laws given of heaven, prescribing rules on spiritual concerns, for faith and worship, both to be answered by man to his Maker.

We believe that rulers, states, and governments have a right, and are bound to enact laws for the protection of all citizens in the free exercise of their religious belief; but we do not believe that they have a right in justice to deprive citizens of this privilege, or proscribe them in their opinions, so long as a regard and reverence are shown to the laws and such religious opinions do not justify sedition nor conspiracy.

We believe that the commission of crime should be punished according to the nature of the offense; that

murder, treason, robbery, theft, and the breach of the
general peace, in all respects, should be punished according to their criminality and their tendency to evil among
men, by the laws of that government in which the offense
is committed; and for the public peace and tranquility all
men should step forward and use their ability in bringing
offenders against good laws to punishment.

We do not believe it just to mingle religious influence
with civil government, whereby one religious society is
fostered and another proscribed in its spiritual privileges,
and the individual rights of its members, as citizens,
denied. . . .

We believe that men should appeal to the civil law for
redress of all wrongs and grievances, where personal
abuse is inflicted or the right of property or character infringed, where such laws exist as will protect the same;
but we believe that all men are justified in defending
themselves, their friends, and property, and the government, from the unlawful assaults and encroachments of all
persons in times of exigency, where immediate appeal
cannot be made to the laws, and relief afforded. (D&C
134:1-9, 11.)

In view of the fact that justice and humanity was denied
Church members by a society that professed to uphold constitutional rights, how could Church leaders continue to
urge the Church members to uphold constitutional government? Two principles—both a result of revelation—need to
be kept in mind.

First, God had promised the Saints protection and blessings if they would live in accordance with all of His commandments which He provided for the establishment of
Zion. These commandments were not followed, particularly
the living of the law of consecration. In a revelation in June
1834, the Lord rebuked the Saints and said that because they
did not "impart their substance, as becometh saints, to the
poor and afflicted among them . . . [they] must needs be
chastened until they learn obedience, . . . *by the things
which they suffer.*" (D&C 105:3, 6; italics added.) With revelation as an indication to their character flaws, they regarded
persecution as God's chastisement upon them.

But there was a second principle that involved their appeals for redress. The Constitution of the United States formed a government based on law. The law provided for redress and reparation when there was a deprivation of rights. By commandment, members of the Church were to uphold constitutional law, and to use it—not retaliation—as a means of redress. If injustices occurred, as they did with the early members of the Church, God would "vex the nation." President Joseph Fielding Smith wrote that "when the Saints . . . were denied their civil and religious rights, those officials were left without excuse, and the judgments of the Almighty which *later came upon them during the Civil War,* were justified."[20]

In the latter part of the nineteenth century, when plural marriage was practiced, the federal government disenfranchised the Church and confiscated all of its property valued at over $50,000. Under the circumstances of this persecution, President Wilford Woodruff received the following revelation on November 24, 1889:

> I the Lord hold the destiny of the Courts in your midst, and the destiny of this nation, and all other nations of the earth in mine own hands; all that I have revealed, and promised and decreed concerning the generation in which you live, shall come to pass, and no power shall stay my hand. . . . If the Saints will hearken unto my voice, and the counsel of my servants, the wicked shall not prevail. Let my servants, who officiate as your Counselors before the Courts, make their pleadings as they are moved upon by the Holy Spirit, without any further pledges from the Priesthood, and they shall be justified. *I the Lord will hold the Courts, with the officers of government, and the nation responsible for their acts towards the inhabitants of Zion.* I, Jesus Christ, the savior of the world, am in your midst. I am your advocate with the Father. . . . Search the Scriptures, for they are they which testify of me; also those revelations which I have given to my Servant Joseph, and to all my Servants since the world began, which are recorded in the records of divine truth. Those revelations contain the judgments of God, which are to be poured out upon all nations under the heavens,

which include great babylon. These judgments are at the
door, they will be fulfilled as God lives. Leave judgment
with me, it is mine saith the Lord.[21]

The persistent counsel of the Lord to Latter-day Saints is
to uphold constitutional law, and, if injustices occur, to use
the courts of the land to resolve the injustices. If justice is
not received through these appeals, the Lord will hold the
officers of the court responsible. In this manner, every
person is made accountable before the Lord.

The Constitution of the United States is regarded by The
Church of Jesus Christ of Latter-day Saints as a fundamental
part of its religious belief. Why? Because it guarantees freedom of religion and holds people accountable to preserve
the rights of every person according to "just and holy principles." Contained in the Constitution is the proviso that
"Congress shall make no law respecting an establishment of
religion, or prohibiting the free exercise thereof." That is a
guarantee to every man and woman. Therefore, the members of the Church have duties as citizens to see that they
use their influence "to keep church and state separated, to
sustain civil power in its appropriate realm, and to stipulate
in constitutions, in legislative enactments, in executive
decrees, in judicial determinations, in every possible way,
that men are free to worship as they will and not be subject
to compulsion."[22]

Only with the government of the United States has there
been such a guarantee of religious freedom, but, as we have
seen with the example of one religious body, when evil
people violate this right to worship, they place not only
themselves under the judgment of Almighty God, but the
nation as well.

To paraphrase the Prophet Joseph Smith's statement
during his imprisonment in Liberty Jail, "None but fools will
trifle with the [rights] of men."[23]

"Let Us Become a Virtuous People"

> If we would most truly enjoy the gift of Heaven, let us become a virtuous people; then shall we both deserve and enjoy it. While, on the other hand, if we are universally vicious and debauched in our manners, though the form of our Constitution carries the face of the most exalted freedom, we shall in reality be the most abject slaves.
>
> *Samuel Adams*

The genius of constitutionalism as devised under the American system is that it created a republican form of government that guaranteed the states a government by representatives who would be elected by the people. Both the representatives and the people are thereby accountable before God for their actions. Revelation to the Prophet Joseph Smith in 1833 prescribed that the Constitution "should be maintained for the rights and protection of all flesh, according to just and holy principles; . . . *that every man may be accountable for his own sins in the day of judgment.*" (D&C 101:77-78; italics added.)

How was liberty to be preserved under the new Constitution? In the minds of the founders, it depended on the virtue and wisdom of both the elected and the electorate. Gordon Wood, prize-winning historian, provided this insight into the eighteenth-century perspective:

> In a republic, . . . each man must somehow be persuaded to submerge his personal wants into the greater

good of the whole. This willingness of the individual to
sacrifice his private interests for the good of the community—such patriotism or love of country—the eigh-
teenth century termed "public virtue." A republic was
such a delicate polity precisely because it demanded an
extraordinary moral character in the people. Every state in
which the people participated needed a degree of virtue;
*but a republic which rested solely on the people abso-
lutely required it.* Although a particular structural arrangement of the government in a republic might temper the
necessity for public virtue, ultimately "no model of government whatever can equal the importance of this principle, nor afford proper safety and security without it."

"Without some portion of this generous principle,
anarchy and confusion would immediately ensue, the jar-
ring interests of individuals, regarding themselves only,
and indifferent to the welfare of others, would still further
heighten the distressing scene, and with the assistance of
the selfish passions, it would end in the ruin and subver-
sion of the state." The eighteenth-century mind was thoroughly convinced that a popularly based government
"cannot be supported without *Virtue.*" Only with a
public-spirited, self-sacrificing people could the authority
of a popularly elected ruler be obeyed, but "more by the
virtue of the people, than by the terror of his power."
Because virtue was truly the lifeblood of the republic, the
thoughts and hopes surrounding this concept of public
spirit gave the Revolution its socially radical character—
an expected alteration in the very behavior of the people,
"laying the foundation in a constitution, not without or
over, but within the subjects."[1]

Virtue in the minds of the founders meant placing the
interest of country before the interest of self. Frugality,
industry, temperance, and good moral character were essential characteristics to maintain the spirit of unity and solidar-
ity among the nation. Recognized was the fact that there
could be no republic without virtue. Unvirtuous character,
which seeks its own interests, was regarded as inimical to
the republic because it neglected the good of the whole
people. Garry Wills has suggested that we cannot histor-

ically explain America without understanding "the code of public virtue espoused without embarrassment by its most distinguished leaders."[2]

So let us consider the testimonials of a few of the most distinguished leaders as they espoused the code.

George Washington:

> The general Government . . . can never be in danger of degenerating into a . . . despotic or oppressive form, so long as there shall remain any virtue in the body of the People.[3]

> There is no truth more thoroughly established, than that there exists in the economy and course of nature, an indissoluble union between virtue and happiness, between duty and advantage, between the genuine maxims of an honest and magnanimous policy, and the solid rewards of public prosperity and felicity.[4]

John Adams:

> Statesmen . . . may plan and speculate for Liberty, but it is Religion and Morality alone, which can establish the Principles upon which Freedom can securely stand. . . . The only foundation of a free Constitution, is pure Virtue, and if this cannot be inspired into our People, in a greater Measure, than they have it now, They may change their Rulers, and the forms of Government, but they will not obtain a lasting Liberty.[5]

On another occasion, Adams wrote: "Liberty can no more exist without virtue and independence, than the body can live and move without a soul."[6] The Constitution, he emphasized, "was made only for a moral and religious people. It is wholly inadequate to the government of any other."[7]

James Madison:

> The aim of every political constitution is, or ought to be, first to obtain for rulers men who possess most wisdom to discern, and most virtue to pursue, the com-

mon good of the society; and in the next place, to take the most effectual precautions for keeping them virtuous whilst they continue to hold their public trust.[8]

Later in the Virginia Ratifying Convention he said:

Is there no virtue among us? If there be not, we are in a wretched situation. No theoretical checks, no form of government, can render us secure. To suppose that any form of government will secure liberty or happiness without any virtue in the people, is a chimerical idea. If there be sufficient virtue and intelligence in the community, it will be exercised in the selection of these men; so that we do not depend upon *their* virtue, or put confidence in our *rulers,* but in the *people* who are to choose them.[9]

Alexander Hamilton:

The institution of delegated power implies that there is a portion of virtue and honor among mankind, which may be a reasonable foundation of confidence.[10]

Was the view unrealistic that virtuous individuals would serve the interest of their community and nation? Garry Wills answers:

Perhaps. But extraordinary men made the vision a reality, at least for a while. They were a privileged few, but they insisted on honest performance within their meritocracy. The most virtuous man *did* lead Virginia into war—Peyton Randolph. The most virtuous man *did* conduct that war and form the nation and rule it without Napoleonic excess—George Washington. A galaxy of distinguished men devoted themselves to public service, and launched the first new nation of the Enlightenment, the first successful modern republic formed on a rational plan. States *did* surrender their sovereignty to form a nobler whole. We cannot suppose the experiment they understood was bound to succeed. What kept us from falling back into monarchy, as France did after her great burst of revolutionary energy? Madison would not have hesitated one minute in answering that question. The public virtue kept us republican. It is the only thing that can.[11]

But why does Wills belabor the point that public virtue was so imbedded in the founders' consciousness? Because today, Americans "do not even pretend [to] choose . . . politicians for their virtue. That kind of talk would look sappy or insincere in our political discourse. But it was no such thing for Madison and his contemporaries. . . . Without him and his like, without their ideals, their virtuous labors for the common good, there would have been no America to be preserved and passed on through the necessary changes of the centuries."[12]

A republic preserved by the virtue of an electorate and the elected—that was the grand view of the founders! And no one better represented the reasoning behind their perspective than Virginia's Richard Henry Lee, who said, "A virtuous people make just laws, and good laws tend to preserve unchanged a virtuous people. A virtuous and happy people by laws uncongenial to their characters, may easily be gradually changed into servile and depraved creatures."[13]

The founders' view about virtue in the electorate was consistent with a revelation, given to Joseph Smith in August 1833, wherein the Saints were enjoined to diligently seek out honest, wise, and good people and then uphold them in public office. (See D&C 98:10.)

Why only the virtuous in public office? Virtuous representatives will act with the public interest and not their own. They will not display a "fervid but false solicitude for the unfortunate" in order to garner votes. They are willing to sacrifice self-interest and their own ideas for the good of society. This was one of the grand achievements of the Philadelphia Convention. The most eminent of the statesmen submerged their own views in the interest of the federal constitution.

Franklin, the eldest among the delegates, urged others to sign with this petition: "I consent, Sir, to this Constitution because I expect no better, and because I am not sure, that it is not the best. The opinions I have had of its errors, I sacrifice to the public good."[14]

Hamilton echoed the same sentiment: "No man's ideas were more remote from the plan than his were known to be;

but is it possible to deliberate between anarchy and Convulsion on one side, and the chance of good to be expected from the plan on the other."[15] Virtue in leaders presupposes an allegiance to law higher than human legislation. Virtuous leaders not only recognize principles that are immutably constant (whereas human laws are not), but those principles are their lodestar. "There never was yet a truly great man," said Franklin, "who was not at the same time truly virtuous."

But in a republic, moral government requires more than public virtue; it requires private virtue among the electorate. Indeed, virtue is a primary responsibility of the people. To require public virtue of the elected without private virtue in its citizens is to require something that cannot be. An unvirtuous electorate will hardly elect a virtuous legislature. As Franklin pointed out: "Only a virtuous people are capable of freedom. As nations become corrupt and vicious, they have more need of masters."[16]

Self-government implies self-mastery.

Private virtue (honesty, frugality, self-reliance, industry, chastity) can only result when there are choices between good and evil, and the people have the freedom to act and freely express their choices. Representative government is therefore a system preferable to others because it permits people to act according "to the moral agency" given to them, so that "every man may be accountable for his own sins in the day of judgment." (D&C 101:78.) People are deprived of that accountability under despotic or dictatorial systems. This point was made clear in the Book of Mormon, in a discourse by King Mosiah.

Following the family (patriarchal) government initiated by Lehi, the Nephites consecrated Nephi as king. A succession of monarchs followed down through Mosiah II. But when each of Mosiah's sons refused to succeed him, the system of government among the Nephites was changed to elected judges. After the first election of judges, Mosiah counseled his people on the preferred system of government and gave the reasons for it.

Monarchial rule was disadvantageous because monarchs can give capricious, unrighteous law; their judgments are "not always just," and they can create much iniquity. (See Mosiah 29:7, 12, 17, and 23.) The prime example of an unrighteous monarch in Nephite history was King Noah. Using him as an example, Mosiah said that the only way an evil king can be dethroned is through revolution, which causes much bloodshed.

In contrast to a monarchy, elected judges represent the voice of the people, and "it is not common that the voice of the people desireth anything contrary to that which is right." Therefore, the commendable government, advised by King Mosiah, was "to do your business by the voice of the people." (Mosiah 29:26.) If judges do not judge equitably, they may be overturned by higher judges. The strength of the system was that "every man may enjoy his rights and privileges alike." (Mosiah 29:32.)

But the greatest merit of the system of judges is that the burden of virtue was on the people. They had to choose wise judges who would judge according to the laws of God. In this way, the people were accountable for their own sins. (See Mosiah 29:38.)

The essentiality of personal righteousness to the preservation of good government is a repeated theme throughout the Book of Mormon. The book is a testimonial that those nations that do not keep the commandments of God are doomed to destruction. Both the Jaredite and Nephite nations were destroyed because of their failure to obey the divine decree—worship the God of this land or be swept off!

The Book of Mormon, however, is more than a record of a fallen people; it is addressed to the latter-day Gentile nation—the current inhabitants of North and South America. Our tenancy on the "land of promise" remains as conditional as that of the Nephites and Jaredites: we must serve God or we shall be "swept off."

> We can behold the decrees of God concerning this land, that it is a land of promise; and whatsoever nation

shall possess it shall serve God, or they shall be swept off when the fulness of his wrath shall come upon them. And the fulness of his wrath cometh upon them when they are ripened in iniquity.

For behold, this is a land which is choice above all other lands; wherefore he that doth possess it shall serve God or shall be swept off; for it is the everlasting decree of God. And it is not until the fulness of iniquity among the children of the land, that they are swept off.

And this cometh unto you, O ye Gentiles, that ye may know the decrees of God—that ye may repent, and not continue in your iniquities until the fulness come, that ye may not bring down the fulness of the wrath of God upon you as the inhabitants of the land have hitherto done.

Behold, this is a choice land, and whatsoever nation shall possess it shall be free from bondage, and from captivity, and from all other nations under heaven, if they will but serve the God of the land, who is Jesus Christ, who hath been manifested by the things which we have written. (Ether 2:9-12.)

The quality of virtue required of the citizens is also specified in the Book of Mormon:

Turn, all ye Gentiles, from your wicked ways; and repent of your evil doings, of your lyings and deceivings, and of your whoredoms, and of your secret abominations, and your idolatries, and of your murders, and your priestcrafts, and your envyings, and your strifes, and from all your wickedness and abominations, and come unto me, and be baptized in my name, that ye may receive a remission of your sins, and be filled with the Holy Ghost, that ye may be numbered with my people who are of the house of Israel. (3 Nephi 30:2.)

Righteousness and personal virtue are not just noble ideals; they are imperative to the republic's survival. Why? Because the people must be dedicated to sustain law higher than their own to make government work. If they cease to sustain the principle of law, the republic will collapse by anarchy. A republic demands an extraordinary character from its citizens to make it work.

Some argue, "What I do in my private life is of no consequence to anyone else." Scripturally, that argument is false.
One's actions add to the collective virtue or vice of the
nation. Every person's goodness adds to the collective righteousness of the nation; every person's sin diminishes that
righteousness. The public virtue is but an emanation of the
private virtue of every individual.

What then of the state of American morality today? Evi-
dence of the moral decline in America is everywhere present: gambling, drinking, and premarital sex, all condemned
under God's laws, are easily rationalized under an
"anything-I-want-to-do-is-right" ethic. Our basic integrity is
suspect when one out of four Americans admits to cheating
on tax returns and many young people show a permissive
attitude toward lying and stealing. It is estimated that Americans "steal" about 160 billion dollars each year from em-
ployers, by arriving late, leaving early, or misusing time on
the job.[17]

America is a nation concerned with out-of-wedlock
births, but illegitimacy, not immorality, is seen as the problem. In the 1960s, federal statistics indicated that about half
of the women surveyed said they had experienced sex
before marriage. Today, more than 80 percent report sexual
experience before marriage. Sixty-one percent reportedly
regard premarital sex as not wrong.[18]

Drug use has reached epidemic proportions. The *U.S.
News* poll reported that 20 percent of young adults had
experimented with cocaine and that half under the age of
thirty had tried marijuana.[19]

The problems are abetted by the sensational treatment
of violence and sexuality in films, literature, television,
video, and theater. Greed and cynicism among athletes,
politicians, and executives show youth that their eccentric
life-style is acceptable behavior. Eliminated from the public-
school curriculum is almost any effort to teach fundamental
values of honesty, integrity, and morality, or that the nation
was founded on Christian beliefs and standards. Today, the
mention of personal virtue is seen as a threat to others'

liberty. So today, if "young Americans are shaped, they are unfortunately shaped to be moral neuters"[20] because the inculcation of basic moral principles has ceased as a part of American education.

This secularization of the American school system has contributed to a deplorable outcome: We have matriculated a generation of Americans who live as if they are accountable to no one but themselves and their own perceived needs. Certainly many feel no accountability to God. In place of absolute moral standards to guide behavior is the conventional ethic that whatever society and courts of law permit is all right. The result is a vague, ambiguous generality of what constitutes right and wrong. Our sense of virtue has been blunted by the hysteria and propaganda of the image-makers who would have us believe that the caricature they portray as "the good life" is an accurate picture of all society. That, of course, is a supreme lie that, if believed, will lead this nation—as it has others—to its death.

So how can we prevent such an outcome? Only by doing as Samuel Adams and others of the early founders said: by becoming a virtuous people! By worshiping the God of this land, Jesus Christ, and by accepting His teachings as our standard of moral judgments and behavior. When we do this, we shall share in the perception of those who devised the Constitution, which gives us a form of government under which every person is "accountable [to God] for his own sins in the day of judgment." (D&C 101:78.)

With the divine appointment of President Ezra Taft Benson as prophet, seer, and revelator to The Church of Jesus Christ of Latter-day Saints, significant to all members was his maiden message for our time: Repent, cleanse the inner vessel, study the Book of Mormon and heed its teachings, and forsake the sin of the Nephites—personal pride.[21]

As we do so, we will uphold the "just and holy principles" that undergird our Constitution and thereby save ourselves, our families, and our nation.

Appendix 1

The First Presidency Statement on the Constitution, 1973

In preparation for the Bicentennial of the United States, the First Presidency of The Church of Jesus Christ of Latter-day Saints, Harold B. Lee, N. Eldon Tanner, and Marion G. Romney, issued the following statement in 1973:

> We urge members of the Church and all Americans to begin now to reflect more intently on the meaning and importance of the Constitution, and of adherence to its principles, in giving strength not only to this country but to the entire family of nations.
>
> In these challenging days, when there are so many influences which would divert us, there is a need to re-dedicate ourselves to the lofty principles and practices of our founding fathers. While we must never permit an erosion of the freedoms the Constitution guarantees, we cannot let permissiveness replace responsibility.
>
> The late President J. Reuben Clark, an eminent scholar in Constitutional law and for many years a member of the First Presidency, said 33 years ago:
>
> "It [the Constitution] gave us, for perhaps the first time in all history, a republic with the three basic divisions of government—the legislative, executive, and judicial—mutually, and completely independent the one from the other, under which it is not possible for any branch of government legally to set up a system by which that branch can first conceive what it wants to do, then make the law ordering its doing, and then, itself, judge its own enforcement of its own law, a system that has always brought extortion, oppression, intimidation, tyranny,

despotism—a system that every dictator has employed and must employ."

There must be a dedication to observing and honoring the law of the land. To remain strong, we must cherish chastity and fidelity, love of work, personal integrity, and the desire to serve our fellow men. We must always remember that God rules in the affairs of men, and that he is truly the Heavenly Father of all mankind. We are all brothers and sisters.

No priority should come before responsible parenthood. No unit needs continual strengthening more than the family.

Under the blessings of liberty secured by the Constitution, we must continue to pursue excellence and progress, but we must recognize that to move forward we must ever hold fast to those moral laws of the Lord which do not change.

On this anniversary day we invite men and women everywhere to join us in the inspired prayer of a modern prophet: "Have mercy, O Lord, upon all the nations of the earth; have mercy on the rulers of our land; may those principles, which were so honorably and nobly defended, namely, the Constitution of our land, by our fathers, be established forever." (D&C 109:54.) (*Ensign,* November 1973, p. 90.)

The Declaration of Independence

IN CONGRESS, July 4, 1776.
A DECLARATION
By the REPRESENTATIVES of the
UNITED STATES OF AMERICA,
In GENERAL CONGRESS assembled

When in the Course of human Events, it becomes necessary for one People to dissolve the Political Bands which have connected them with another, and to assume among the Powers of the Earth, the separate and equal Station to which the Laws of Nature and of Nature's God entitle them, a decent Respect to the Opinions of Mankind requires that they should declare the causes which impel them to the Separation.

We hold these Truths to be self-evident, that all Men are created equal, that they are endowed by their Creator with certain unalienable Rights, that among these are Life, Liberty, and the Pursuit of Happiness—That to secure these Rights, Governments are instituted among Men, deriving their just Powers from the Consent of the Governed, that whenever any Form of Government becomes destructive of these Ends, it is the Right of the People to alter or to abolish it, and to institute new Government, laying its Foundation on such Principles, and organizing its Powers in such Form, as to them shall seem most likely to effect their Safety and Happiness. Prudence, indeed, will dictate that Governments long established should not be changed for light and transient Causes; and accordingly all Experience hath shewn, that Mankind are more disposed to suffer, while Evils are sufferable, than to right themselves by abolishing the Forms to which they are accustomed. But when a long Train of Abuses and Usurpations, pursuing invariably the same Object, evinces a Design to reduce them under absolute Despotism, it is their Right, it is their Duty, to throw off such Government, and to provide new Guards for their future Security. Such has been the patient Sufferance of these Colonies; and such is now the Necessity which constrains them to alter their former Systems of Government. The History of the present King of Great-Britain is a History of repeated Injuries and Usurpations, all having in direct Object the Establishment of an absolute Tyranny over these States. To prove this, let Facts be submitted to a candid World.

He has refused his Assent to Laws, the most wholesome and necessary for the public Good.

He has forbidden his Governors to pass Laws of immediate and pressing Importance, unless suspended in their Operation till his Assent should be obtained; and when so suspended, he has utterly neglected to attend to them.

He has refused to pass other Laws for the Accommodation of large Districts of People, unless those People would relinquish the Right of Representation in the Legislature, a Right inestimable to them, and formidable to Tyrants only.

He has called together Legislative Bodies at Places unusual, uncomfortable, and distant from the Depository of their Public Records, for the sole Purpose of fatiguing them into Compliance with his Measures.

He has dissolved Representative Houses repeatedly, for opposing with manly Firmness his Invasions on the Rights of the People.

He has refused for a long Time, after such Dissolutions, to cause others to be elected; whereby the Legislative Powers, incapable of Annihilation, have returned to the People at large for their exercise; the State remaining in the mean time exposed to all the Dangers of Invasion from without, and Convulsions within.

He has endeavoured to prevent the Population of these States; for that Purpose obstructing the Laws for Naturalization of Foreigners; refusing to pass others to encourage their Migrations hither, and raising the Conditions of new Appropriations of Lands.

He has obstructed the Administration of Justice, by refusing his Assent to Laws for establishing Judiciary Powers.

He has made Judges dependent on his Will alone, for the

Tenure of their Offices, and the Amount and payment of their Salaries.

He has erected a Multitude of new Offices, and sent hither Swarms of Officers to harrass our People, and eat out their Substance.

He has kept among us, in Times of Peace, Standing Armies, without the consent of our Legislatures.

He has affected to render the Military independent of, and superior to the Civil Power.

He has combined with others to subject us to a Jurisdiction foreign to our Constitution, and unacknowledged by our Laws; giving his Assent to their Acts of pretended Legislation:

For quartering large Bodies of Armed Troops among us:

For protecting them, by a mock Trial, from Punishment for any Murders which they should commit on the Inhabitants of these States:

For cutting off our Trade with all Parts of the World:

For imposing Taxes on us without our Consent:

For depriving us, in many Cases, of the Benefits of Trial by Jury:

For transporting us beyond Seas to be tried for pretended Offences:

For abolishing the free System of English Laws in a neighbouring Province, establishing therein an arbitrary Government, and enlarging its Boundaries, so as to render it at once an Example and fit Instrument for introducing the same absolute Rule into these Colonies:

For taking away our Charters, abolishing our most valuable Laws, and altering fundamentally the Forms of our Governments:

For suspending our own Legislatures, and declaring themselves invested with Power to legislate for us in all Cases whatsoever.

He has abdicated Government here, by declaring us out of his Protection and waging War against us.

He has plundered our Seas, ravaged our Coasts, burnt our towns, and destroyed the Lives of our People.

He is, at this Time, transporting large Armies of foreign Mercenaries to compleat the works of Death, Desolation, and Tyranny, already begun with circumstances of Cruelty and Perfidy, scarcely paralleled in the most barbarous Ages, and totally unworthy the Head of a civilized Nation.

He has constrained our fellow Citizens taken Captive on the high Seas to bear Arms against their Country, to become the Executioners of their Friends and Brethren, or to fall themselves by their Hands.

He has excited domestic Insurrections amongst us, and has endeavoured to bring on the Inhabitants of our Frontiers, the merciless Indian Savages, whose known Rule of Warfare, is an undistinguished Destruction, of all Ages, Sexes and Conditions.

In every stage of these Oppressions we have Petitioned for Redress in the most humble Terms: Our repeated Petitions have been answered only by repeated Injury. A Prince, whose Character is thus marked by every act which may define a Tyrant, is unfit to be the Ruler of a free People.

Nor have we been wanting in Attention to our British Brethren. We have warned them from Time to Time of Attempts by their Legislature to extend an unwarrantable Jurisdiction over us. We have reminded them of the Circumstances of our Emigration and Settlement here. We have appealed to their native Justice and Magnanimity, and we have conjured them by the Ties of our common Kindred to disavow these Usurpations, which, would inevitably interrupt our Connections and Correspondence. They too have been deaf to the Voice of Justice and of Consanguinity. We must, therefore, acquiesce in the Necessity, which denounces our Separation, and hold them, as we hold the rest of Mankind, Enemies in War, in Peace, Friends.

We, therefore, the Representatives of the UNITED STATES OF AMERICA, in General Congress, Assembled, appealing to the Supreme Judge of the World for the Rectitude of our Intentions, do, in the Name, and by Authority of the good People of these Colonies, solemnly Publish and Declare, That these United Colonies are, and of Right ought to be, Free and Independent States; that they are absolved from all Allegiance to the British Crown, and that all political Connection between them and the State of Great-Britain, is and ought to be totally dissolved; and that as Free and Independent States, they have full Power to levy War, conclude Peace, contract Alliances, establish Commerce, and to do all other Acts and Things which Independent States may of right do. And for the support of this declaration, with a firm Reliance on the Protection of divine Providence, we mutually pledge to each other our lives, our Fortunes, and our sacred Honor.

Appendix 3

The Constitution

WE THE PEOPLE of the United States, in Order to form a more perfect Union, establish Justice, insure domestic Tranquility, provide for the common Defence, promote the general Welfare, and secure the Blessings of Liberty to ourselves and our Posterity, do ordain and establish this CONSTITUTION for the United States of America.

Article I

Section 1

All legislative Powers herein granted shall be vested in a Congress of the United States, which shall consist of a Senate and House of Representatives.

Section 2

The House of Representatives shall be composed of Members chosen every second Year by the People of the several States, and the Electors in each State shall have the Qualifications requisite for Electors of the most numerous Branch of the State Legislature.

No Person shall be a Representative who shall not have attained to the Age of twenty-five Years, and been seven Years a Citizen of the United States, and who shall not, when elected, be an Inhabitant of that State in which he shall be chosen.

[Representatives and direct Taxes shall be apportioned among the several States which may be included within this Union, according to their respective Numbers, which shall be determined by adding to the whole Number of free Persons, including those bound to Service for a Term of Years, and excluding Indians not taxed, three fifths of all other Persons.]* The actual Enumeration shall be made within three Years after the first Meeting of the Congress of the United States and within every subsequent Term of ten Years, in such Manner as they shall by Law direct. The Number of Representatives shall not exceed one for every thirty Thousand, but each State shall have at Least

---

*Superseded by the fourteenth amendment.

one Representative; and until such enumeration shall be made, the State of New Hampshire shall be entitled to chuse three, Massachusetts eight, Rhode-Island and Providence Plantations one, Connecticut five, New-York six, New Jersey four, Pennsylvania eight, Delaware one, Maryland six, Virginia ten, North Carolina five, South Carolina five, and Georgia three.

When vacancies happen in the Representation from any State, the Executive Authority thereof shall issue Writs of Election to fill such Vacancies.

The House of Representatives shall chuse their Speaker and other Officers; and shall have the sole Power of Impeachment.

Section 3

The Senate of the United States shall be composed of two Senators from each State, [chosen by the Legislature thereof,]* for six Years; and each Senator shall have one Vote.

Immediately after they shall be assembled in Consequence of the first Election, they shall be divided as equally as may be into three Classes. The Seats of the Senators of the first Class shall be vacated at the Expiration of the second Year, of the second Class at the Expiration of the fourth Year, and of the third Class at the Expiration of the sixth Year, so that one-third may be chosen every second Year; [and if Vacancies happen by Resignation, or otherwise, during the Recess of the Legislature of any State, the Executive thereof may make temporary Appointments until the next Meeting of the Legislature, which shall then fill such Vacancies.]**

No Person shall be a Senator who shall not have attained to the Age of thirty Years, and been nine Years a Citizen of the United States, and who shall not, when elected, be an Inhabitant of that State for which he shall be chosen.

The Vice President of the United States shall be President of the Senate, but shall have no Vote, unless they be equally divided.

The Senate shall chuse their other Officers, and also a President pro tempore, in the absence of the Vice President, or when he shall exercise the Office of President of the United States.

The Senate shall have the sole Power to try all Impeachments. When sitting for that Purpose, they shall be on Oath or

*Superseded by the seventeenth amendment.

**Modified by the seventeenth amendment.

Affirmation. When the President of the United States is tried, the Chief Justice shall preside: And no Person shall be convicted without the Concurrence of two thirds of the Members present.

Judgment in Cases of Impeachment shall not extend further than to removal from Office, and disqualification to hold and enjoy any Office of honor, Trust or Profit under the United States: but the Party convicted shall nevertheless be liable and subject to Indictment, Trial, Judgment and Punishment, according to Law.

Section 4

The Times, Places and Manner of holding Elections for Senators and Representatives, shall be prescribed in each State by the Legislature thereof; but the Congress may at any time by Law make or alter such Regulations, except as to the Place of Chusing Senators.

[The Congress shall assemble at least once in every Year, and such Meeting shall be on the first Monday in December, unless they shall by Law appoint a different Day.] *

Section 5

Each House shall be the Judge of the Elections, Returns and Qualifications of its own Members, and a Majority of each shall constitute a Quorum to do Business; but a smaller number may adjourn from day to day, and may be authorized to compel the Attendance of absent Members, in such Manner, and under such Penalties as each House may provide.

Each House may determine the Rules of its Proceedings, punish its Members for disorderly Behavior, and, with the Concurrence of two thirds, expel a Member.

Each House shall keep a Journal of its Proceedings, and from time to time publish the same, excepting such Parts as may in their Judgment require Secrecy; and the Yeas and Nays of the Members of either House on any question shall, at the Desire of one fifth of those Present, be entered on the Journal.

Neither House, during the Session of Congress, shall, without the Consent of the other, adjourn for more than three days, nor to any other Place than that in which the two Houses shall be sitting.

Section 6

The Senators and Representatives shall receive a Compensation for their Services, to be ascertained by Law, and paid out

---

*Superseded by the twentieth amendment.

of the Treasury of the United States. They shall in all Cases, except Treason, Felony and Breach of the Peace, be privileged from Arrest during their Attendance at the Session of their respective Houses, and in going to and returning from the same; and for any Speech or Debate in either House, they shall not be questioned in any other Place.

No Senator or Representative shall, during the Time for which he was elected, be appointed to any civil Office under the Authority of the United States, which shall have been created, or the Emoluments whereof shall have been encreased during such time; and no Person holding any Office under the United States, shall be a Member of either House during his Continuance in Office.

Section 7

All Bills for raising Revenue shall originate in the House of Representatives; but the Senate may propose or concur with Amendments as on other Bills.

Every Bill which shall have passed the House of Representatives and the Senate, shall, before it become a Law, be presented to the President of the United States; If he approve he shall sign it, but if not he shall return it, with his Objections to that House in which it shall have originated, who shall enter the Objections at large on their journal, and proceed to reconsider it. If after such Reconsideration two thirds of that House shall agree to pass the Bill, it shall be sent, together with the Objections, to the other House, by which it shall likewise be reconsidered, and if approved by two thirds of that House, it shall become a Law. But in all such Cases the Votes of both Houses shall be determined by Yeas and Nays, and the Names of the Persons voting for and against the Bill shall be entered on the Journal of each House respectively. If any Bill shall not be returned by the President within ten Days (Sundays excepted) after it shall have been presented to him, the Same shall be a Law, in like Manner as if he had signed it, unless the Congress by their Adjournment prevent its Return, in which Case it shall not be a Law.

Every Order, Resolution, or Vote to which the Concurrence of the Senate and House of Representatives may be necessary (except on a question of Adjournment) shall be presented to the President of the United States; and before the Same shall take Effect, shall be approved by him, or being disapproved by him, shall be repassed by two thirds of the Senate and House of Representatives, according to the Rules and Limitations prescribed in the Case of a Bill.

Section 8

The Congress shall have Power To lay and collect Taxes, Duties, Imposts and Excises, to pay the Debts and provide for the common Defence and general Welfare of the United States; but all Duties, Imposts and Excises shall be uniform throughout the United States;

To borrow money on the credit of the United States;

To regulate Commerce with foreign Nations, and among the several States, and with the Indian Tribes;

To establish an uniform Rule of Naturalization, and uniform Laws on the subject of Bankruptcies throughout the United States;

To coin Money, regulate the Value thereof, and of foreign Coin, and fix the Standard of Weights and Measures;

To provide for the Punishment of counterfeiting the Securities and current Coin of the United States;

To establish Post Offices and post Roads;

To promote the Progress of Science and useful Arts, by securing for limited Times to Authors and Inventors the exclusive Right to their respective Writings and Discoveries;

To constitute Tribunals inferior to the supreme Court;

To define and punish Piracies and Felonies committed on the high Seas, and Offenses against the Law of Nations;

To declare War, grant Letters of Marque and Reprisal, and make Rules concerning Captures on Land and Water;

To raise and support Armies, but no Appropriation of Money to that Use shall be for a longer Term than two Years;

To provide and maintain a Navy;

To make Rules for the Government and Regulation of the land and naval Forces;

To provide for calling forth the Militia to execute the Laws of the Union, suppress Insurrections and repel Invasions;

To provide for organizing, arming, and disciplining the Militia, and for governing such Part of them as may be employed in the Service of the United States, reserving to the States respectively, the Appointment of the Officers, and the Authority of training the Militia according to the discipline prescribed by Congress;

To exercise exclusive Legislation in all Cases whatsoever,

over such District (not exceeding ten Miles square) as may, by Cession of particular States, and the acceptance of Congress, become the Seat of the Government of the United States, and to exercise like Authority over all Places purchased by the Consent of the Legislature of the State in which the Same shall be, for the Erection of Forts, Magazines, Arsenals, dock-Yards, and other needful Buildings;—And

To make all Laws which shall be necessary and proper for carrying into Execution the foregoing Powers, and all other Powers vested by this Constitution in the Government of the United States, or in any Department or Officer thereof.

Section 9

The Migration or Importation of such Persons as any of the States now existing shall think proper to admit, shall not be prohibited by the Congress prior to the Year one thousand eight hundred and eight, but a tax or duty may be imposed on such Importations, not exceeding ten dollars for each Person.

The privilege of the Writ of Habeas Corpus shall not be suspended, unless when in Cases of Rebellion or Invasion the public Safety may require it.

No Bill of Attainder or ex post facto Law shall be passed.

No capitation, or other direct, Tax shall be laid, unless in Proportion to the Census or Enumeration herein before directed to be taken. *

No Tax or Duty shall be laid on Articles exported from any State.

No Preference shall be given by any Regulation of Commerce or Revenue to the Ports of one State over those of another: nor shall Vessels bound to, or from, one State, be obliged to enter, clear, or pay Duties in another.

No Money shall be drawn from the Treasury, but in Consequence of Appropriations made by Law; and a regular Statement and Account of the Receipts and Expenditures of all public Money shall be published from time to time.

No Title of Nobility shall be granted by the United States: And no Person holding any Office of Profit or Trust under them, shall, without the Consent of the Congress, accept of any present, Emolument, Office, or Title, of any kind whatever, from any King, Prince, or foreign State.

---

*Modified by the sixteenth amendment.

Section 10

No State shall enter into any Treaty, Alliance, or Confederation; grant Letters of Marque and Reprisal; coin Money; emit Bills of Credit; make any Thing but gold and silver Coin a Tender in Payment of Debts; pass any Bill of Attainder, ex post facto Law, or Law impairing the Obligation of Contracts, or grant any Title of Nobility.

No State shall, without the Consent of the Congress, lay any Imposts or Duties on Imports or Exports, except what may be absolutely necessary for executing its inspection Laws; and the net Produce of all Duties and Imposts, laid by any State on Imports or Exports, shall be for the Use of the Treasury of the United States; and all such Laws shall be subject to the Revision and Control of the Congress.

No State shall, without the Consent of Congress, lay any duty of Tonnage, keep Troops, or Ships of War in time of Peace, enter into any Agreement or Compact with another State, or with a foreign Power, or engage in War, unless actually invaded, or in such imminent Danger as will not admit of delay.

Article II

Section 1

The executive Power shall be vested in a President of the United States of America. He shall hold his Office during the Term of four Years, and, together with the Vice-President, chosen for the same Term, be elected, as follows

Each State shall appoint, in such Manner as the Legislature thereof may direct, a Number of Electors, equal to the whole Number of Senators and Representatives to which the State may be entitled in the Congress: but no Senator or Representative, or Person holding an Office of Trust or Profit under the United States, shall be appointed an Elector.·

[The Electors shall meet in their respective States, and vote by Ballot for two persons, of whom one at least shall not be an Inhabitant of the same State with themselves. And they shall make a List of all the Persons voted for, and of the Number of Votes for each; which List they shall sign and certify, and transmit sealed to the Seat of the Government of the United States, directed to the President of the Senate. The President of the Senate shall, in the Presence of the Senate and House of Representatives, open all the Certificates, and the Votes shall then be counted. The Person having the greatest Number of

Votes shall be the President, if such Number be a Majority of the whole Number of Electors appointed; and if there be more than one who have such Majority, and have an equal Number of Votes, then the House of Representatives shall immediately chuse by Ballot one of them for President; and if no Person have a Majority, then from the five highest on the List the said House shall in like Manner chuse the President. But in chusing the President, the Votes shall be taken by States, the Representation from each State having one Vote; A quorum for this Purpose shall consist of a Member or Members from two-thirds of the States, and a Majority of all the States shall be necessary to a Choice. In every Case, after the Choice of the President, the Person having the greatest Number of Votes of the Electors shall be the Vice President. But if there should remain two or more who have equal Votes, the Senate shall chuse from them by Ballot the Vice-President.] *

The Congress may determine the Time of chusing the Electors, and the Day on which they shall give their Votes; which Day shall be the same throughout the United States.

No person except a natural born Citizen, or a Citizen of the United States, at the time of the Adoption of this Constitution, shall be eligible to the Office of President; neither shall any Person be eligible to that Office who shall not have attained to the Age of thirty-five Years, and been fourteen Years a Resident within the United States.

In Case of the Removal of the President from Office, or of his Death, Resignation, or Inability to discharge the Powers and Duties of the said Office, * * the same shall devolve on the Vice President, and the Congress may by Law provide for the Case of Removal, Death, Resignation or Inability, both of the President and Vice President, declaring what Officer shall then act as President, and such Officer shall act accordingly, until the Disability be removed, or a President shall be elected.

The President shall, at stated Times, receive for his Services, a Compensation, which shall neither be encreased nor diminished during the Period for which he shall have been elected, and he shall not receive within that Period any other Emolument from the United States, or any of them.

Before he enter on the Execution of his Office, he shall take the following Oath or Affirmation:—"I do solemnly swear (or

---

* Superseded by the twelfth amendment.

* * Modified by the twenty-fifth amendment.

affirm) that I will faithfully execute the Office of President of the United States, and will to the best of my Ability, preserve, protect and defend the Constitution of the United States."

Section 2

The President shall be Commander in Chief of the Army and Navy of the United States, and of the Militia of the several States, when called into the actual Service of the United States; he may require the Opinion in writing, of the principal Officer in each of the executive Departments, upon any subject relating to the Duties of their respective Offices, and he shall have Power to Grant Reprieves and Pardons for Offenses against the United States, except in Cases of Impeachment.

He shall have Power, by and with the Advice and Consent of the Senate, to make Treaties, provided two-thirds of the Senators present concur; and he shall nominate, and by and with the Advice and Consent of the Senate, shall appoint Ambassadors, other public Ministers and Consuls, Judges of the supreme Court, and all other Officers of the United States, whose Appointments are not herein otherwise provided for, and which shall be established by Law; but the Congress may by Law vest the Appointment of such inferior Officers, as they think proper, in the President alone, in the Courts of Law, or in the Heads of Departments.

The President shall have Power to fill up all Vacancies that may happen during the Recess of the Senate, by granting Commissions which shall expire at the End of their next Session.

Section 3

He shall from time to time give to the Congress Information of the State of the Union, and recommend to their Consideration such Measures as he shall judge necessary and expedient; he may, on extraordinary Occasions, convene both Houses, or either of them, and in Case of Disagreement between them, with Respect to the Time of Adjournment, he may adjourn them to such Time as he shall think proper; he shall receive Ambassadors and other public Ministers; he shall take Care that the Laws be faithfully executed, and shall Commission all the Officers of the United States.

Section 4

The President, Vice President and all civil Officers of the United States, shall be removed from Office on Impeachment for, and Conviction of, Treason, Bribery, or other high Crimes and Misdemeanors.

124

Article III

Section 1

The judicial Power of the United States, shall be vested in one supreme Court, and in such inferior Courts as the Congress may from time to time ordain and establish. The Judges, both of the supreme and inferior Courts, shall hold their Offices during good Behavior, and shall, at stated Times, receive for their Services a Compensation which shall not be diminished during their Continuance in Office.

Section 2

The judicial Power shall extend to all Cases, in Law and Equity, arising under this Constitution, the Laws of the United States, and Treaties made, or which shall be made, under their Authority;—to all Cases affecting Ambassadors, other public Ministers and Consuls;—to all Cases of admiralty and maritime Jurisdiction;—to Controversies to which the United States shall be a Party;—to Controversies between two or more States;—between a State and Citizens of another State;*—between Citizens of different States;—between Citizens of the same State claiming Lands under Grants of different States, and between a State, or the Citizens thereof, and foreign States, Citizens or Subjects.

In all Cases affecting Ambassadors, other Public Ministers and Consuls, and those in which a State shall be Party, the supreme Court shall have original Jurisdiction. In all the other Cases before mentioned, the supreme Court shall have appellate Jurisdiction, both as to Law and Fact, with such Exceptions, and under such Regulations as the Congress shall make.

The trial of all Crimes, except in Cases of Impeachment, shall be by Jury; and such Trial shall be held in the State where the said Crimes shall have been committed; but when not committed within any State, the Trial shall be at such Place or Places as the Congress may by Law have directed.

Section 3

Treason against the United States, shall consist only in levying War against them, or in adhering to their Enemies, giving them Aid and Comfort. No Person shall be convicted of Treason unless on the Testimony of two Witnesses to the same overt Act, or on Confession in open Court.

The Congress shall have power to declare the Punishment of

*Modified by the eleventh amendment.

Treason, but no Attainder of Treason shall work Corruption of Blood, or Forfeiture except during the Life of the Person attained.

Article IV

Section 1

Full Faith and Credit shall be given in each State to the public Acts, Records, and judicial Proceedings of every other State. And the Congress may by general Laws prescribe the Manner in which such Acts, Records and Proceedings shall be proved, and the Effect thereof.

Section 2

The Citizens of each State shall be entitled to all Privileges and Immunities of Citizens in the several States.

A Person charged in any State with Treason, Felony, or other Crime, who shall flee from Justice, and be found in another State, shall on demand of the executive Authority of the State from which he fled, be delivered up, to be removed to the State having Jurisdiction of the Crime.

[No Person held to Service or Labour in one State, under the Laws thereof, escaping into another, shall, in Consequence of any Law or Regulation therein, be discharged from such Service or Labour, but shall be delivered up on Claim of the Party to whom such Service or Labour may be due.]*

Section 3

New States may be admitted by the Congress into this Union; but no new State shall be formed or erected within the Jurisdiction of any other State; nor any State be formed by the Junction of two or more States, or parts of States, without the Consent of the Legislatures of the States concerned as well as of the Congress.

The Congress shall have Power to dispose of and make all needful Rules and Regulations respecting the Territory or other Property belonging to the United States; and nothing in this Constitution shall be so construed as to Prejudice any Claims of the United States, or of any particular State.

Section 4

The United States shall guarantee to every State in this Union a Republican Form of Government, and shall protect each of them against Invasion; and on Application of the Legislature, or

---

*Superseded by the thirteenth amendment.

of the Executive (when the Legislature cannot be convened) against domestic Violence.

Article V

The Congress, whenever two-thirds of both Houses shall deem it necessary, shall propose Amendments to this Constitution, or, on the Application of the Legislatures of two-thirds of the several States, shall call a Convention for proposing Amendments, which, in either Case, shall be valid to all Intents and Purposes, as part of this Constitution, when ratified by the Legislatures of three-fourths of the several States, or by Conventions in three-fourths thereof, as the one or the other Mode of Ratification may be proposed by the Congress; Provided that no Amendment which may be made prior to the Year One thousand eight hundred and eight shall in any Manner affect the first and fourth Clauses in the Ninth Section of the first Article; and that no State, without its Consent, shall be deprived of its equal Suffrage in the Senate.

Article VI

All Debts contracted and Engagements entered into, before the Adoption of this Constitution, shall be as valid against the United States under this Constitution, as under the Confederation.

This Constitution, and the Laws of the United States which shall be made in Pursuance thereof; and all Treaties made, or which shall be made, under the Authority of the United States, shall be the supreme Law of the Land; and the Judges in every State shall be bound thereby, any Thing in the Constitution or Laws of any State to the Contrary notwithstanding.

The Senators and Representatives before mentioned, and the Members of the several State Legislatures, and all executive and judicial Officers, both of the United States and of the several States, shall be bound by Oath or Affirmation, to support this Constitution; but no religious Test shall ever be required as a Qualification to any Office or public Trust under the United States.

Article VII

The Ratification of the Conventions of nine States shall be sufficient for the Establishment of this Constitution between the States so ratifying the Same.

DONE in Convention by the Unanimous Consent of the States present the Seventeenth Day of September in the Year of our Lord one thousand seven hundred and Eighty seven and of the Independence of the United States of America the Twelfth. In Witness whereof We have hereunto subscribed our Names.

BILL OF RIGHTS*

The Conventions of a number of the States having, at the time of their adopting the Constitution, expressed a desire, in order to prevent misconstruction or abuse of its powers, that further declaratory and restrictive clauses should be added: And as extending the ground of public confidence in the Government, will best insure the beneficent ends of its institution:

Resolved, by the SENATE and HOUSE OF REPRESENTATIVES of the UNITED STATES of AMERICA in Congress assembled, two thirds of both Houses concurring. That the following Articles be proposed to the Legislatures of the several States, as Amendments to the Constitution of the United States; all, or any of which articles, when ratified by three fourths of the said Legislatures, to be valid to all intents and purposes, as part of the said Constitution, viz.

Articles in addition to, and Amendment of the Constitution of the United States of America, proposed by Congress, and ratified by the Legislatures of the several States, pursuant to the fifth Article of the Original Constitution.

Article 1

After the first enumeration required by the first Article of the Constitution, there shall be one Representative for every thirty thousand, until the number shall amount to one hundred, after which, the proportion shall be so regulated by Congress, that there shall be not less than one hundred Representatives, nor less than one Representative for every forty thousand persons, until the number of Representatives shall amount to two hundred, after which, the proportion shall be so regulated by Congress,

---

*These are the original twelve amendments submitted by Congress. Only the last ten were ratified. The Bill of Rights amendments were ratified on December 15, 1791.

that there shall not be less than two hundred Representatives, nor more than one Representative for every fifty thousand persons. [Not Ratified]

Article 2

No law, varying the compensation for the services of the Senators and Representatives, shall take effect, until an election of Representatives shall have intervened. [Not Ratified]

Article 3

Congress shall make no law respecting an establishment of religion, or prohibiting the free exercise thereof; or abridging the freedom of speech, or of the press; or the right of the people peaceably to assemble, and to petition the Government for a redress of grievances. [Amendment 1]

Article 4

A well regulated Militia, being necessary to the security of a free State, the right of the people to keep and bear Arms, shall not be infringed. [Amendment 2]

Article 5

No Soldier shall, in time of peace, be quartered in any house, without the consent of the owner, nor in time of war, but in a manner to be prescribed by law. [Amendment 3]

Article 6

The right of the people to be secure in their persons, houses, papers, and effects, against unreasonable searches and seizures, shall not be violated, and no Warrants shall issue but upon probable cause, supported by oath or affirmation, and particularly describing the place to be searched, and the persons or things to be seized. [Amendment 4]

Article 7

No person shall be held to answer for a capital, or otherwise infamous crime, unless on a presentment or indictment of a grand jury, except in cases arising in the land or Naval forces, or in the Militia, when in actual service in time of War or public danger; nor shall any person be subject for the same offence to be twice put in jeopardy of life or limb; nor shall be compelled in any criminal case, to be a witness against himself, nor be deprived of life, liberty, or property, without due process of law; nor shall private property be taken for public use without just compensation. [Amendment 5]

Article 8

In all criminal prosecutions, the accused shall enjoy the right to a speedy and public trial by an impartial jury of the State and district wherein the crime shall have been committed, which district shall have been previously ascertained by law, and to be informed of the nature and cause of the accusation; to be confronted with the witnesses against him; to have compulsory process for obtaining witnesses in his favor, and to have the assistance of counsel for his defence. [Amendment 6]

Article 9

In suits at common law, where the value in controversy shall exceed twenty dollars, the right of trial by jury shall be preserved, and no fact, tried by a jury, shall be otherwise reexamined in any Court of the United States, than according to the rules of the common law. [Amendment 7]

Article 10

Excessive bail shall not be required, nor excessive fines imposed, nor cruel and unusual punishments inflicted. [Amendment 8]

Article 11

The enumeration in the Constitution, of certain rights, shall not be construed to deny or disparage others retained by the people. [Amendment 9]

Article 12

The powers not delegated to the United States by the Constitution, nor prohibited by it to the States, are reserved to the States respectively, or to the people. [Amendment 10]

Appendix 4

The Thirty-nine Signers
of the Constitution

Signer	Born	Died (Age at Death)	Occupation
1. Abraham Baldwin (Georgia)	22 Nov 1754	4 Mar 1807 (52)	Lawyer
2. Richard Bassett (Delaware)	2 Apr 1745	15 Sep 1815 (70)	Lawyer
3. Gunning Bedford, Jr. (Delaware)	1747	30 Mar 1812 (64)	Lawyer
4. John Blair (Virginia)	1732	31 Aug 1800 (68)	Lawyer
5. William Blount (North Carolina)	26 Mar 1749	21 Mar 1800 (50)	Politician
6. David Brearley (New Jersey)	11 Jun 1745	16 Aug 1790 (45)	Lawyer

Education	Age at Signing	Interesting Facts About the Signer
Yale	32	Founded University of Georgia. U. S. congressman 1789-1799. U. S. senator 1799-1807.
	42	Favored strong national government. Senator 1789-1793. Governor of Delaware 1799-1800. Appointed federal circuit judge 1801.
College of New Jersey (Princeton)	40	Aide-de-camp to General George Washington in Revolutionary War. Classmate at Princeton of James Madison. U. S. district court judge for Delaware 1789-1812.
William and Mary; Middle Temple in London	55	Originally opposed Patrick Henry's resolution against the Stamp Act, but later joined with him. President Washington appointed him an associate justice of the first Supreme Court.
	38	First man ever impeached by U. S. House of Representatives and expelled from U. S. Senate for conspiracy and land fraud. Died in disgrace.
	42	Served as officer in Revolutionary War. Ardent Episcopalian, helped compile *The Book of Common Prayer*. Appointed by Washington as District Judge for New Jersey.

Signer	Born	Died (Age at Death)	Occupation
7. Jacob Broom (Delaware)	1752	25 Apr 1810 (58)	Businessman
8. Pierce Butler (South Carolina)	11 Jul 1744	15 Feb 1822 (77)	Soldier Planter
9. Daniel Carroll II (Maryland)	22 Jul 1730	7 May 1796 (65)	Landowner
10. George Clymer (Pennsylvania)	16 Mar 1739	23 Jan 1813 (73)	Banker
11. Jonathan Dayton (New Jersey)	16 Oct 1760	9 Oct 1824 (63)	Lawyer
12. John Dickinson (Delaware)	8 Nov 1732	14 Feb 1808 (75)	Lawyer

Education	Age at Signing	Interesting Facts About the Signer
	35	Greatest contribution was his appeal during the convention that delegates must agree on some new plan of government, even if by a bare majority. The convention was on the verge of breaking up, and his appeal seemed to cause the delegates to continue forward.
	42	Strong spokesman for Southern slaveholders. Believed that the number of representatives from each state should be based on wealth of state, not population. U. S. senator from South Carolina.
Educated in France	56	Wealthy landowner and merchant. Signed the Articles of Confederation and the Constitution. Member of U. S. House of Representatives 1789-1791. Believed the Constitution was the "best form of government which has ever been offered to the world."
College of Philadelphia (University of Pennsylvania)	48	One of the signers of the Declaration of Independence. Served as U. S. Representative 1789-1791.
College of New Jersey (Princeton)	26	Youngest man to sign the Constitution. Served as officer in Revolutionary War. Served as U. S. Representative 1791-1799; Speaker in House of Representatives 1795-1799. U. S. senator 1799-1805. Indicted for treason with Arron Burr but never brought to trial.
Studied law in England	54	Distinguished lawyer, called the "Penman of the Revolution" because of the documents he wrote. Drafted the Articles of Confederation and helped write the Constitution. He refused to sign the Declaration of Independence.

Signer	Born	Died (Age at Death)	Occupation
13. William Few (Georgia)	8 Jun 1748	16 Jul 1828 (80)	Politician
14. Thomas FitzSimons (Pennsylvania)	1741	26 Aug 1811 (64)	Businessman
15. Benjamin Franklin (Pennsylvania)	17 Jan 1706	17 Apr 1790 (84)	Publisher
16. Nicholas Gilman (New Hampshire)	3 Aug 1755	2 May 1814 (58)	Politician
17. Nathaniel Gorham (Massachusetts)	27 May 1738	11 Jun 1796 (58)	Businessman
18. Alexander Hamilton (New York)	11 Jan 1755/ 1757	12 Jul 1804 (47 or 49)	Lawyer
19. Jared Ingersoll (Pennsylvania)	27 Oct 1749	31 Oct 1822 (73)	Lawyer
20. Daniel of St. Thomas Jenifer (Maryland)	1723	16 Nov 1790 (67)	Landowner

Education	Age at Signing	Interesting Facts About the Signer
	39	U. S. Senator 1789-1793. Self-educated. Moved to New York, where he was elected to the New York Legislature.
	46	First Roman Catholic to be elected to public office in Pennsylvania. Captain in Revolutionary War. Favored property ownership for voting in congressional elections. U. S. congressman 1789-1795.
	81	Oldest to sign the Constitution. Signer of the Declaration of Independence. Favored a unicameral legislature. Petitioned for prayer during convention.
	32	Served as officer in Revolutionary War. U. S. Representative in Congress 1789-1797. U. S. senator 1805-1814.
	51	Important role in writing of the Constitution. Opposed limiting voting rights to property owners. In later life, suffered financial reverses that contributed to his death.
Kings College (Columbia University)	30/32	Officer in Revolutionary War. Collaborated with Jay and Madison in writing *The Federalist* papers. Died of wound from duel with Arron Burr. Wanted Washington to be king. First secretary of treasury under Washington.
Yale	38	Unsuccessfully ran for vice-president on the Federalist Party ticket. Attorney general of Pennsylvania 1790-1799. Died a poor man because of western property speculation.
	64	Bachelor, wealthy aristocrat, and friend of George Washington. Served during Revolutionary War. Not an original delegate but was substitute when others refused to serve.

Signer	Born	Died (Age at Death)	Occupation
21. William Samuel Johnson (Connecticut)	7 Oct 1727	14 Nov 1819 (92)	Lawyer-educator
22. Rufus King (Massachusetts)	24 Mar 1755	29 Apr 1827 (72)	Lawyer
23. John Langdon (New Hampshire)	25 Jun 1741	18 Sep 1819 (78)	Shipowner
24. William Livingston (New Jersey)	30 Nov 1723	25 Jul 1790 (66)	Lawyer
25. James Madison, Jr. (Virginia)	16 Mar 1751	28 Jun 1836 (85)	Politician

Education	Age at Signing	Interesting Facts About the Signer
Yale	59	Originally did not support the idea of American independence during the Revolutionary War but later signed the Constitution. President of Columbia College 1789-1800. U. S. senator 1789-1791.
Harvard	32	Helped write the Constitution. Was twice the Federalist Party's unsuccessful candidate for vice-president and once for president. Served under six presidents. Twice U. S. senator 1789-1796, 1813-1825. Twice U. S. minister to Great Britain.
	46	A wealthy man. Helped finance American Revolution by building first American warship, *Ranger*. Raised New Hampshire troops in 1777. Fought in Revolutionary War. Paid expenses for himself and fellow delegate to Constitutional Convention. First president pro tempore of Senate. Counted first electoral votes and informed Washington of his election as president. U. S. senator 1789-1801. Governor of New Hampshire 1805-09; 1810-12.
Yale	63	Fought in Revolution. Member of powerful and wealthy family. Won fame as writer of political essays. First governor of New Jersey 1776-1790.
College of New Jersey (Princeton)	36	"Father of the Constitution" at age 36. He kept the most complete account of the convention. Wrote many of *The Federalist* essays. Member of Congress 1789-1797. Secretary of state 1801-1809. Fourth president of the U. S. 1809-1817.

Signer	Born	Died (Age at Death)	Occupation
26. James McHenry (Maryland)	16 Nov 1753	3 May 1816 (62)	Physician
27. Thomas Mifflin (Pennsylvania)	10 Jan 1744	20 Jan 1800 (56)	Politician
28. Gouverneur Morris (Pennsylvania)	31 Jan 1752	16 Nov 1816 (64)	Lawyer
29. Robert Morris (Pennsylvania)	31 Jul 1734	8 May 1806 (72)	Financier
30. William Paterson (New Jersey)	24 Dec 1745	9 Sep 1806 (61)	Lawyer
31. Charles Pinckney (South Carolina)	26 Oct 1757	29 Oct 1824 (67)	Lawyer

Education	Age at Signing	Interesting Facts About the Signer
	33	Fought during Revolutionary War. Taken prisoner by British. Became secretary and aide to Washington. Appointed by Washington as secretary of war; also by Adams 1796-1800.
College of Pennsylvania (University of Pennsylvania)	43	Served as Washington's first aide-de-camp in Revolutionary War. Achieved rank of major general. Helped write the Constitution. Governor of Pennsylvania 1790-1799.
Kings College (Columbia University)	35	An accomplished orator, he gave more speeches at the convention than any other man. Wrote Constitution in its final form. U. S. minister to France. U. S. senator 1800-1803.
	53	Signer of the Declaration of Independence. One of the wealthiest men in the United States. Pledged his credit to finance supplies during the war. U. S. senator 1789-1795. Later lost his fortune in western land speculation and was jailed for his debts.
College of New Jersey (Princeton)	42	Authored provisions of the Constitution. Governor of New Jersey. U. S. senator 1789-1790. Associate Justice of Supreme Court 1793-1806.
Middle Temple in London	29	Captain in Revolutionary War. Prisoner of war to British. Author of so-called Pinckney plan during the convention. Responsible for many provisions on the drafted Constitution. Three times governor of South Carolina. U. S. senator 1798-1801. U. S. representative in Congress 1819-1821.

Signer	Born	Died (Age at Death)	Occupation
32. Charles Cotesworth Pinckney (South Carolina)	25 Feb 1746	16 Aug 1825 (79)	Lawyer
33. George Read (Delaware)	18 Sep 1733	21 Sep 1798 (65)	Lawyer
34. John Rutledge (South Carolina)	1739	18 Jul 1800 (61)	Lawyer
35. Roger Sherman (Connecticut)	19 Apr 1721	23 Jul 1793 (72)	Merchant Lawyer
36. Richard Dobbs Spaight (North Carolina)	25 Mar 1758	6 Sep 1802 (44)	Politician
37. George Washington (Virginia)	22 Feb 1732	14 Dec 1799 (67)	Planter

Education	Age at Signing	Interesting Facts About the Signer
Educated in England— Oxford and Middle Temple in London	41	Brigadier general during Revolutionary War. Prisoner to the British. Helped write the Constitution. Major general and third in command in new U. S. Army 1798-1800. Unsuccessful Federalist Party candidate for vice-president. Twice ran unsuccessfully for president.
	53	A signer of the Declaration of Independence. Preferred strong, central government. U. S. senator 1789-93. Chief justice of Delaware 1793-1798.
Middle Temple in London	48	Distinguished lawyer whose knowledge was used in drafting the Constitution. Associate justice of Supreme Court 1789-1791. Chief justice, South Carolina. Acting chief justice U. S. Supreme Court 1795. U. S. Senate refused to confirm appointment.
	66	A signer of the Declaration of Independence. Also signed the Articles of Confederation. Member of U. S. Congress 1789-91. U. S. senator 1791-1793. Regarded slavery as "iniquitous."
University of Glasgow	29	Officer in Revolutionary War. Governor of North Carolina 1792-1795. Member of Congress 1798-1801. Died of wounds at age 44 after duel with another congressman.
	55	Commander in chief of Continental Army. Presiding officer at Constitutional Convention. First president of U. S. 1789-1797. Jefferson said of him, "His integrity was most pure, his justice the most inflexible I have ever known, no motives or consanguinity, of friendship or hatred being able to bias his decision. He was indeed . . . a wise, a good and great man. . . . On the whole, his character was . . . perfect, in nothing bad."

Signer	Born	Died (Age at Death)	Occupation
38. Hugh Williamson (North Carolina)	5 Dec 1735	22 May 1819 (73)	Physician
39. James Wilson (Pennsylvania)	14 Sep 1742	21 Aug 1798 (55)	Lawyer

Education	Age at Signing	Interesting Facts About the Signer
College of Pennsylvania (University of Pennsylvania)	51	An outstanding scholar and scientist. Served in war as a surgeon general. First representative from North Carolina to U. S. Congress 1790-1793.
University of Edinburgh	44	A signer of the Declaration of Independence. Frequently read speeches of Benjamin Franklin during the convention. Strongly opposed wealth as criterion for representation. Associate justice of Supreme Court 1789-1798.

Notes

Prologue

1. For a discussion on the meaning of an inspired Constitution, see Richard L. Bushman, "Inspired Constitution," *Brigham Young University Studies* 4 (Winter 1962):159-63; Noel B. Reynolds, "The Doctrine of An Inspired Constitution" *Brigham Young University Studies* 3 (Spring 1976):315-40; Rex E. Lee, "The United States Constitution: Divinity and Controversy," Commissioner's Lecture Series (Provo, Utah: Brigham Young University Press, 1972). Bushman and Reynolds argue that the inspiration of the Constitution consists in the principles that provide for the rights and protection of all flesh. Lee emphasizes that the guiding hand of Deity is not only in various provisions of the document but in the "total grand concept and overall structure" of the document.

Many latter-day prophets have equated the Constitution to scripture. For example, President George Albert Smith said, "The Constitution of the United States of America is just as much from my Heavenly Father as the Ten Commandments." (*Conference Report,* April 1948, p. 182.) President J. Reuben Clark, Jr., declared, "It is my conviction that God inspired the inditing of that document. Thus the Constitution becomes sacred scripture to me." ("Gratitude For Our Heritage," Harold B. Lee Library, Special Collections, Brigham Young University, no date, pp. 10-11.) And again President Clark said, "The Constitution of the United States is to me and to my people as much a part of our religion as the Decalogue . . . or the Beatitudes." (*Vital Speeches of the Day,* January 1, 1939, vol. 5, no. 6, p. 177.) President Ezra Taft Benson has written, "I reverence the Constitution of the United States as a sacred document. To me its words are akin to the revelations of God, for God has placed His stamp of approval on the Constitution of this land." (Ezra Taft Benson, *The Constitution—A Heavenly Banner* [Salt Lake City: Deseret Book Company, 1986], p. 31.)

Do these statements mean that every provision in the Constitution is the inerrant word of the Lord? Obviously not, for the original document sanctioned slavery, whereas a revelation of the Lord said that "it is not right that any man should be in bondage one to another." (D&C 101:79.) The sacredness and inspiration of the document is in the God-inspired principles that secure the liberty of all mankind.

2. President Brigham Young said that the Prophet Joseph Smith declared, "The time will come when the destiny of the nation will hang by a single thread. At that critical juncture, this people will step forth and save it from the threatened destruction." (*Journal of Discourses,* 26 vols. [London: Latter-day Saints' Book Depot, 1854-86], 7:15.) Elder Orson Hyde remembered the Prophet's statement as follows: "I believe he said something like this—that the time would come when the Constitution and the country would be in danger of overthrow; and said he: 'If the Constitution be saved at all, it will be by the Elders of this Church.' I believe this is about the language, as nearly as I can recollect it." (*Journal of Discourses* 6:152.) James Burgess recorded, "In the month of May 1843. Several miles east of Nauvoo. The Nauvoo Legion was on parade and review. At the close

of which Joseph Smith made some remarks upon our condition as a people and upon our future prospects contrasting our present condition with our past trials and persecutions by the hands of our enemies. Also upon the constitution and government of the United States stating that the time would come when the Constitution and Government would hang by a *brittle* thread and would be ready to fall into other hands but this people the Latter day Saints will step forth and save it. General Scott and part of his staff on the American Army was present on the occasion. I James Burgess was present and testify to the above." (Andrew F. Ehat and Lyndon W. Cook, editors and compilers, *The Words of Joseph Smith* [Provo, Utah: Brigham Young University, 1980], p. 279.) Earlier, on July 19, 1840, Joseph Smith said, "Even this nation will be on the very verge of crumbling to pieces and tumbling to the ground and when the Constitution is upon the brink of ruin this people will be the staff up[on] which the nation shall lean and they shall tear the Constitution away from the very verge of destruction." (Historical Department, The Church of Jesus Christ of Latter-day Saints, Salt Lake City, Utah.)

3. *Journal of Discourses* 26:39.

4. J. Reuben Clark, Jr., said in 1959, "In the past 61 years, . . . I have given 125 addresses . . . on the Constitution of the United States, its virtues, and the evils of socialism. That has been my theme for lo, these 60 years." (*Deseret News,* July 25, 1959.) His speeches and excerpts are chronicled in J. Reuben Clark, *Stand Fast by Our Constitution* (Salt Lake City: Deseret Book Company, 1973) and J. Reuben Clark, Jr., *J. Reuben Clark Selected Papers,* edited by David H. Yarn, Jr. (Provo, Utah: Brigham Young University Press, 1984).

5. Professor Edwin Corwin's classic analysis of the evolution of Supreme Court decisions noted four distinguishable periods in the court's interpretations of the document: first, the dominance of the document itself, where it and the testimony of *The Federalist* was used as the basis of interpretation (1790 to 1835); second, the idea that the court was an arbiter between two sovereign powers— the national and state governments (1835 to 1895); third, the period of judicial flexibility epitomized by the expression of one judge that "the Constitution is what the Supreme Court says it is" (1895 to 1917); and fourth (from about 1917 to 1955), a permissiveness toward the aggregation of power flowing to the executive and legislative branches. Corwin concluded: "What was once vaunted as a Constitution of Rights, both state rights and private rights, has been replaced to a great extent by a Constitution of Powers." (*The Constitution of the United States of America, Analysis and Interpretation* [U. S. Government Printing Office, 1953], pp. xvi-xxxiii.)

Professor Corwin's analysis, while valid, extended only to the 1950s. Since that time, another distinguishable period has developed, which is popularly called judicial activism or judicial legislation. This recent development is the belief that judges do not restrain themselves from imposing their personal biases and private legislation through their decisions.

The courts do make law whenever they interpret legislation. Most interpretations, as Dallin H. Oaks has pointed out, are legitimate judicial lawmaking, but some are not. The only practical remedy to the problem is judicial restraint. For an excellent discussion on the problem of judicial legislation and its remedies, see Rex E. Lee, *A Lawyer Looks at the Constitution* (Provo, Utah: Brigham Young University Press, 1981), pp. 36-38; chapters 17 and 18. Dallin H. Oaks and J. Clifford Wallace provide two brief essays on the problem in *Views from the Bench,* edited by Mark W. Cannon and David M. O'Brien (Chatham, New Jersey: Chatham House Publishers, 1985), pp. 147-54; 155-65. A scholarly approach to the problem is Dallin H. Oaks, "Judicial Activism," *Harvard Journal of Law and Public Policy,* vol. 7, no. 1 (Winter), 1984.

6. *Journal of Discourses* 21:8.

7. See 3 Nephi 16:10-16; 20:14-16; 21:11-23. The Prophet Joseph Smith revealed in 1839 a vision he had received of the last days: "The time is soon coming, when no man will have any peace but in Zion and her stakes.

"I saw men hunting the lives of their own sons, and brother murdering brother, women killing their own daughters, and daughters seeking the lives of their mothers. I saw armies arrayed against armies. I saw blood, desolation, fires. The Son of Man has said that the mother shall be against the daughter, and the daughter against the mother. These things are at our doors. They will follow the Saints of God from city to city. Satan will rage, and the spirit of the devil is now enraged. I know not how soon these things will take place; but with a view of them, shall I cry peace? No; I will lift up my voice and testify of them.

"How long you will have good crops, and the famine be kept off, I do not know; when the fig tree leaves, know then that the summer is nigh at hand." (*Teachings of the Prophet Joseph Smith* [Salt Lake City: Deseret Book Company, 1938], p. 161.)

8. President Charles Penrose said: "The principles of that great instrument [the Constitution] are to go forth to the nations, and the time will come when they will prevail, just as sure as the sun shines even when it appears to be in darkness and the clouds are over it." (*Conference Report,* April 1917, p. 20.)

9. J. Reuben Clark, Jr., *J. Reuben Clark Selected Papers,* pp. 41-42. That the principles of the Constitution would influence other nations' governmental systems is, according to President Harold B. Lee, a fulfillment of prophecy: "I have often wondered what that expression meant, that out of Zion shall go forth the law. Years ago I went with the brethren to the Idaho Falls Temple, and I heard in that inspired prayer of the First Presidency a definition of the meaning of that term 'out of Zion shall go forth the law.' Note what they said: 'We thank thee that thou hast revealed to us that those who gave us our constitutional form of government were men wise in thy sight and that thou didst raise them up for the very purpose of putting forth that sacred document [the Constitution of the United States—see D&C 101:80]. . . .

" 'We pray that kings and rulers and the peoples of all nations under heaven may be persuaded of the blessings enjoyed by the people of this land by reason of their freedom and under their guidance and be constrained to adopt similar governmental systems, thus to fulfill the ancient prophecy of Isaiah and Micah that ". . . out of Zion shall go forth the law and the word of the Lord from Jerusalem." ' " (*Improvement Era,* October 1945, p. 564.)

10. See appendix 1 for First Presidency statement.

11. The fundamental principles that preserve the rights of man are specifically discussed in chapter 4.

12. *Conference Report,* October 1952, p. 18.

13. Spencer W. Kimball, "The False Gods We Worship" (*Ensign,* June 1976, pp. 4, 5.)

14. *Journal of Discourses* 26:39.

15. Ibid., 23:266.

Chapter 1

1. *Journal of Discourses*, 26 vols. (London: Latter-day Saints' Book Depot, 1854-86), 19:229.

2. Thirty-two of the thirty-nine signers of the Constitution were baptized by proxy in the Endowment House before the St. George Temple was completed. The others had their proxy ordinance work completed in later years.

3. *Conference Report,* April 1898, pp. 89-90.
4. *Journal of Discourses* 19:229.
5. "August 21, 1877 I Wilford Woodruff went to the Temple of the Lord this morning and was Baptized for 100 persons who were dead including the signers of the Declaration of Independence all except John Hancock and [William Floyd]. I was Baptized for the following names: [names follow]." (Wilford Woodruff Journal, August 19, 21-24, 1877, Historical Department, The Church of Jesus Christ of Latter-day Saints.) Proxy baptisms had been performed for John Hancock and William Floyd in the Endowment House. The proxy work for Martin Van Buren, James Buchanan, and the president who was then living, Ulysses Simpson Grant, was subsequently done.
6. Matthias Cowley, *Wilford Woodruff* (Salt Lake City: Bookcraft, 1964), p. 500.
7. *Conference Report,* April 1898, p. 90.
8. *Conference Report,* April 1957, p. 47.
9. Henry Steele Commager asked: "Who can doubt, for example, that in the crisis of 1774-1783, the American colonies and states enjoyed far more competent leadership than the British Empire?

"The situation is too familiar to rehearse. In the last quarter of the century the new United States—a nation with a white population of less than three million, without a single major city, and wholly lacking in those institutions of organized society or civilization so familiar in Europe—boasted a galaxy of leaders who were quite literally incomparable: Franklin, Washington, Jefferson, Hamilton, John Adams, Samuel Adams, John Jay, James Wilson, George Mason, Benjamin Rush, James Madison, and a dozen others scarcely less distinguished.

"What explains this remarkable outpouring of political leadership, this fertility in the production of statesmen—a fertility unmatched since that day? Was it an historical accident? Was it a peculiar response to the time or the place, or to a combination of the two? Or was it a product of conditions and attitudes that were cultivated and directed to calculated ends, and that can be if not re-created at least paralleled in our time?" ("Leadership in Eighteenth-Century America and Today," *Freedom and Order* [New York: G. Braziller, 1966], pp. 149-50.)
10. Bruce R. McConkie, *A New Witness for the Articles of Faith* (Salt Lake City: Deseret Book Company, 1985), p. 34; see also p. 512.) Elder McConkie wrote: "No two persons are born with the same talents and capacities; no two are rooted in the same soil of circumstances; each is unique. The cares of this world, gold and honor and power and renown, the lusts of the flesh, the chains of past sins, and a thousand other things—all exert their influence upon us. But in the final sense the answer stems back to premortality. We all lived as spirit beings, as children of the Eternal Father, for an infinitely long period of time in the premortal existence. There we developed talents, gifts, and aptitudes; there our capacities and abilities took form; there, by obedience to law, we were endowed with power, in one degree or another, to believe the truth and follow the promptings of the Spirit. And the talent of greatest worth was that of spirituality, for it enables us to hearken to the Holy Spirit and accept that gospel which prepares us for eternal life.

"Men are not born equal. They enter this life with the talents and capacities developed in preexistence."
11. President J. Reuben Clark, Jr., called this principle "spiritual relativity." He explained: "We were not all equal at the beginning; we were not all equal at the Grand Council; we have never been all equal at any time since, and apparently we never shall be. (*Conference Report,* October 1956, p. 84.)

12. Joseph Smith, *Teachings of the Prophet Joseph Smith* (Salt Lake City: Deseret Book Company, 1938), p. 365.

13. *Conference Report,* April 1898, p. 89.

14. See, for example, Acts 17:22-26 and Deuteronomy 32:7-9. For commentary on these passages that reflects Church theology, see Joseph Fielding Smith, *The Way to Perfection* (Salt Lake City: Deseret News Press, 1956), pp. 46-48.

15. J. Reuben Clark, Jr., *Stand Fast by Our Constitution* (Salt Lake City: Deseret Book Company, 1973), p. 136.

16. President J. Reuben Clark, Jr., explained the Justinian Code: "While the absolute power of the Emperor was implicit in the Theodosian Code, it was boldly announced in the Justinian compilations. The Emperor had all legislative, judicial, and executive power in himself.

"The exact words of the Institute containing this declaration read (in translation): 'The constitution of the prince hath also the force of a law; for the people by a law, called lex regia, make a concession to him of their whole power.'

"This principle seems to have been basic to Roman law in the West. . . . It seems that not always was the principle fully operative, but it seems, also, that there never was a time when the executive power, whoever held it, and howsoever it was secured, was not more or less supreme in all the affairs of state— legislative, executive, and judicial.

"Thus it was inevitable that this principle of the autocratic power of the Emperor, the executive, which was basic in the laws of Western and Southern Europe and portions of the Near East for over 2,000 years (sometimes the principle lay dormant, but still there, during the period of the Roman Republics; sometimes it was active, as in the days of the Empire, West and East), should be a vital portion of the warp and woof of the law of continental Europe." Ibid., pp. 141-42.

17. See Harold J. Berman, *The Interaction of Law and Religion* (Nashville: Abingdon Press, 1974), p. 95. Chapter 2, "The Influence of Christianity on the Development of Western Law," is of special interest.

18. John Dickinson said in the constitutional proceedings, "Experience must be our only guide. Reason may mislead us." *Notes of the Debates in the Federal Convention of 1787 Reported by James Madison* (Athens, Ohio: Ohio University Press, 1966), p. 447.

19. *Journal of Discourses* 2:170.

20. Winston Churchill, *A History of the English-Speaking People: The Age of Revolution* (New York: Dodd, Mead & Co., 1962), 3:193-94.

Chapter 2

1. Of interest to Latter-day Saints is the fact that the pages on the Bible that Washington kissed are portions of the pages of the 49th and 50th chapters of Genesis, which contain the blessing of Jacob (Israel) on the head of his son Joseph. The blessing on the head of Joseph has special significance to Latter-day Saints, for Joseph's descendants were promised that their blessings would prevail above the blessings of Jacob's progenitors "unto the utmost bound of the everlasting hills." The Book of Mormon is an account of some of Joseph's descendants who came to a land of everlasting hills (the North and South American continents) and prophesied that others of Joseph's descendants would inhabit the land, become a great people, and build a holy city to the Lord. (See Ether 13:7-10.)

Elder B. H. Roberts thought that Washington's placing his hand on and kissing the pages of the Bible on this particular prophecy was more than coincidental. Said he: "What seems singular in connection with these promises made to Joseph and the account of their partial fulfillment in a portion of his posterity inhabiting America is, that after the nations, composed largely of his descendants, had been destroyed and other peoples from Europe—among whom, however, were also large numbers of the descendants of Joseph through the loins of Ephraim had taken possession of the land, at the formal inauguration of that government whose mission it is to control the destiny of the great continent of America—the land of Joseph—the very first executive chosen for that nation, when being sworn to preserve, protect and defend the constitution of this land which God had inspired men to frame, he placed his hand upon the very page of the Bible containing the blessing pronounced upon the head of Joseph by the Patriarch Jacob, and kissed it in token that he swore by God's holy word that he would preserve inviolate the constitution which God prepared for this land!

"Will men call this merely coincidence? Strange coincidence indeed it is, if that be all that it is. Observe that the forty-ninth chapter of Genesis is near the very first leaves of the Bible, and in laying the book open upon a velvet cushion for the use of one about to make solemn oath upon it, it would naturally be parted near the middle of the volume and not parted at the first few leaves.

"Let others believe all this to be coincidence if they choose, but for my own part there is too much that is significant to assign it to that class of phenomena so conveniently disposed of by calling them coincidents. And I believe that the men who opened the old Masonic Bible at the page containing the blessing of Joseph were unwittingly guided by the powers of heaven, and that the act heralded an era big with promise for the descendants of Joseph—the establishment of a government under which they would eventually attain to the full enjoyment of all that was pronounced upon their great progenitor by the inspired patriarchs, Jacob and Moses." (*Defense of the Faith and the Saints* [Salt Lake City: *Deseret News,* 1907], 1:414-15.)

2. Farewell Address, September 19, 1796, *The Writings of George Washington,* 1745-1799, edited by John C. Fitzpatrick (Washington, D.C.: U. S. Government Printing Office, 1939), 35:229.

3. David Whitney, *Founders of Freedom in America, Signers of the Constitution of the United States* (Chicago: J. G. Ferguson Publishing Company, 1973), p. 203.

4. Ibid., p. 129.

5. *Notes of the Debates in the Federal Convention of 1787 Reported by James Madison* (Athens, Ohio: Ohio University Press, 1966), p. 406.

6. Whitney, *Founders of Freedom,* p. 122.

7. Ibid., p. 167.

8. Quoted in Frank Donavan, *Mr. Madison's Constitution* (New York: Dodd, Mead & Company, 1965), p. 30.

9. *Notes of the Debates,* p. 658.

10. Whitney, *Founders of Freedom,* p. 166.

11. Quoted in Richard B. Morris, *Framing of the Federal Constitution* (Washington, D.C.: U.S. Department of Interior, 1979), p. 46.

12. Whitney, *Founders of Freedom,* p. 157.

13. Ibid., p. 158.

14. Quoted in Donavan, *Mr. Madison's Constitution,* p. 34.

15. Quoted by Adrienne Koch in the introduction to *Notes of the Debates,* p. xvii.

16. Whitney, *Founders of Freedom,* pp. 228-29.

17. Charles A. Beard, *An Economic Interpretation of the Constitution of the*

United States (New York: Macmillan Publishing Co., 1965). Beard's thesis was that the founders of the republic developed the Constitution to protect their own economic ventures and their "class" financially. Claiming that the founders' primary motive was economic, Beard said the founders used force, fraud, and false propaganda to achieve their ends. A devastating critique of Beard's thesis is Robert E. Brown's *Charles Beard and the Constitution: A Critical Analysis of "An Economic Interpretation of the Constitution"* (New Jersey: Princeton University Press, 1956).

18. See Douglas Adair, "The Tenth Federalist Revisited," *William and Mary Quarterly,* 3rd Series, Vol. 8, January 1951, pp. 48-67; Garry Wills, *Explaining America: The Federalist* (New York: Penguin Books, 1981). Both Adair and Wills show that Madison and his Federalist colleagues were motivated by the ideas from Montesquieu and Hume and not the greedy motives to preserve their class or property as Beard had contended.

19. *Notes of the Debates,* p. 19.

Chapter 3

1. "The framers were all advocates of the principle of constitutionalism. According to the principles, constitutions are distinguished from ordinary acts of legislation. They are charters of fundamental laws, drafted by extraordinary assemblages and ratified by special conventions chosen by the people. As supreme law, they cannot be annulled by legislative fiat." (Richard B. Morris, *Framing of the Federal Constitution* [Washington, D.C.: U.S. Department of Interior, 1979], p. 26.)

2. Friedrich Hayek claims that America's contribution to the world is constitutionalism. See especially chapter 12, "The American Contribution: Constitutionalism," *The Constitution of Liberty* (Chicago: Henry Regnery Company, 1972), pp. 176-93.

3. The Articles of Confederation were the result of a motion for independence by Richard Henry Lee of Virginia on June 7, 1776. When the second Continental Congress convened later that year, they approved the motion to prepare a plan for confederation. John Dickinson, Delaware, headed the drafting committee, and they completed their project within a month. On November 15, 1777, the articles were approved by the congress and sent to the states for ratification. Complete ratification did not occur till March 1, 1781.

The Articles of Confederation did accomplish three notable achievements: (1) it made the final peace with Great Britain in 1783; (2) it established a public land policy for the Western-land territory turned over by states that bordered western land and were making claims; and (3) it enacted the 1787 Northwest Ordinance, which established the regulations for government territories and provided policy for their admission as states on the same equal footing as the original thirteen colonies. (See Richard B. Morris, "How America Struggled to Enact a Constitution," *U. S. News and World Report,* March 9, 1981, pp. 61-62.)

4. Circular to the States, June 8, 1783, *Writings of George Washington,* 1745-1799, edited by John C. Fitzpatrick (Washington, D.C.: U.S. Government Printing Office, 1939), 26:488. Quoted in *Maxims of Washington,* collected and arranged by John Frederick Schroeder (Mount Vernon: The Mount Vernon Ladies' Association, 1942), p. 27.

5. *Writings of George Washington* 29:68.

6. Quoted in Frank Donavan, *Mr. Madison's Constitution* (New York: Dodd, Mead & Company, 1965), p. 8.

7. Ibid., p. 39.

8. Madison's *Notes* were published in 1840 after his death. Congress paid $40,000 for the most complete record of the convention proceedings. Adrienne Koch wrote in his introduction to the printing of the *Notes:* "Certainly it is safe to say that the *Notes* will not be surpassed by any other single or combined set, and they will continue to give us the fullest, most literate, and most reliable information on the framing of the Constitution. As Charles Evans Hughes once remarked, we owe to Madison 'the most direct approach to the intention of the makers of the Constitution.' Were we deprived of its account, we would return to what Jared Sparks once complained of as 'such a very skeleton of dry bones with hardly a sinew, muscle, or ligature, to tell that it was a living thing, that it is impossible to ascertain from it the relative standing or prevailing view of any member.' (*Notes of the Debates in the Federal Convention of 1787 Reported by James Madison* (Athens, Ohio: Ohio University Press, 1966), p. xxiii.)

9. Ibid., p. 147.

10. Ibid., pp. 209-10.

11. Ibid., p. 227.

12. Ibid., p. 283.

13. Congress had already faced the issue on slavery. For tax purposes, it counted slaves at 60 percent or three-fifths of their actual numbers. The convention merely voted to keep that ratio both for apportionment and tax purposes.

14. This situation was remedied by the Twelfth Amendment. The amendment was the result of the election of 1800, when the electoral college cast their votes for Jefferson and Burr without distinguishing who should be the president and vice-president. A tie vote resulted, and the House of Representatives elected Jefferson president and Burr vice-president.

15. Quoted in David Whitney, *Founders of Freedom in America, Signers of the Constitution of the United States* (Chicago: J. G. Ferguson Publishing Company, 1973), p. 33.

16. *Notes of the Debates,* p. 652.

17. Ibid., pp. 653-54.

18. Ibid., p. 659.

19. Donavan, *Mr. Madison's Constitution,* pp. 93-94.

20. Garry Wills, *Explaining America: The Federalist* (New York: Penguin Books, 1981), p. xii.

21. "A spirit of accommodation was the basis of the present constitution." George Washington's letter to David Stuart, March 28, 1780, *Writings of George Washington,* 31:29.

22. Joseph Fielding Smith, *The Progress of Man* (Salt Lake City: Genealogical Society of Utah, 1952), pp. 295-96.

Chapter 4

1. J. Reuben Clark, Jr., *Stand Fast by Our Constitution* (Salt Lake City: Deseret Book Company, 1973), pp. 133-50.

2. George A. Peek, Jr., ed., *The Political Writings of John Adams* (New York: The Liberal Arts Press, 1954), p. 96.

3. *The Federalist Papers* (New York: The New American Library of World Literature, 1961), no. 45, p. 292.

4. Ibid., pp. 292-93.

5. Ibid., no. 51, p. 323.

6. Quoted in Jonathan Elliot, comp., *The Debates in the Several State Conventions on the Adoption of the Federal Constitution,* 5 vols. (Philadelphia: J. B. Lippincott Company, 1901), 3:257-58.

7. *Church News,* Nov. 29, 1952, p. 12.

8. John Adams, *The Works of John Adams,* edited by C. F. Adams (Boston: Little, Brown Co., 1851), 5:490.

9. Thomas Jefferson, *Works of Thomas Jefferson,* edited by Paul L. Ford (New York: J. P. Putnam's Sons, 1905), 11:523.

10. "The Constitution was framed in order to protect minorities. That is the purpose of a written Constitution. In order that minorities might be protected in the matter of amendments under our Constitution, the Lord required that the amendments should be made only through the operation of very large majorities —two thirds for action in the Senate, and three-fourths as among the states. This is the inspired, prescribed order." (*J. Reuben Clark, Jr., Selected Papers,* edited by David H. Yarn, Jr., (Provo, Utah: Brigham Young University Press, 1984), p. 165.)

11. *The Federalist Papers,* no. 10, p. 81.

12. Henry Sumner Maine, *Popular Government* (Indianapolis: Liberty Classics, 1976), p. 227.

13. For a discussion of the first amendment, an excellent treatment is Rex E. Lee, *A Lawyer Looks at the Constitution,* chapters 10-13.

14. *The Federalist Papers,* no. 57, p. 353.

15. Massachusetts Bill of Rights, 1780.

16. Ezra Taft Benson, "The Values by Which to Live," *Leaders Magazine,* volume 7, no. 4, October-November 1984, p. 152.

17. Quoted in Hamilton Abert Long, *The American Ideal of 1776* (Philadelphia: Your Heritage Books, 1963), p. 208.

Chapter 5

1. "The whole of America is Zion itself from north to south, and is described by the Prophets, who declare that it is the Zion where the mountain of the Lord should be, and that it should be in the center of the land." (Joseph Smith, *Teachings of the Prophet Joseph Smith* (Salt Lake City: Deseret Book Company, 1938), p. 362.)

2. The phrase is taken from Thomas Jefferson's First Inaugural Address, *The Annals of America,* 23 volumes (Chicago: Encyclopedia Britannica, 1973), 4:145.

3. In 1820, the Northern States had a population of slightly over two million, with 105 members in the House of Representatives. The Southern, or slave states, had 4,485,000 people and 81 representatives.

4. The compromise "forever prohibited" slavery in parts of the Louisiana purchase north of the 36° 30° north latitude, which was the line marking the westward extension of Missouri's southern border. The Missouri Compromise was later repealed in 1854 by the Kansas-Nebraska Act, which allowed states to decide the issue for themselves.

5. Joseph Smith, *History of the Church of Jesus Christ of Latter-day Saints,* 7 vols., 2nd ed. rev., edited by B. H. Roberts (Salt Lake City: The Church of Jesus Christ of Latter-day Saints, 1932-51.) 1:426-27, 437-38.

6. Ibid. 1:393.

7. Ibid. 1:454.

8. Ibid. 3:59.

9. Ibid. 3:157.

10. Ibid. 3:175.

11. Ibid. 3:304.

12. "The total value of the property destroyed in Missouri, which belonged to the Saints, is beyond our knowledge. It was estimated to be not less than two

million dollars, from the time they first settled in that state until their expulsion.
. . . In the appeal made to Congress and the President of the United States, in
1839, the amount of their losses was estimated at two million dollars. Claims
against Missouri for the losses were presented to Congress in the sum of
$1,381,044.00, and this represented only 491 individuals; many others who lost
property, entered no claims for damages against that state." (Joseph Fielding
Smith, *Essentials in Church History* [Salt Lake City: Deseret Book Company,
1973], pp. 209-10.)

13. *History of the Church* 3:332.

14. Ibid. 4:80.

15. Ibid.

16. See *History of the Church* 4:90-92 for the complete statement of the
Congressional Committee's report. After receiving the unfavorable report, the
Church adopted a series of resolutions in the April 1840 general conference that
condemned the congressional report as "unconstitutional" and urged the First
Presidency to "appeal our case to the Court of Heaven." (See *History of the
Church* 4:107-9.)

17. Ibid. 6:56-57.

18. Joseph Fielding Smith made this significant commentary on verse 1:
"Taking this article in its entirety we are willing to accept it, for it contains sound
principles that are acceptable today, and will be approved by the Church until
that day comes when the Rightful Ruler of the earth shall come to set up his
perfect government. One statement in this article, we could modify and give a
better meaning. 'We believe that governments were instituted of God for the
benefit of man,' might be more nearly correct if stated: 'A *perfect* government
was instituted of God for the benefit of man.' The statement that governments, if
this is interpreted to mean all governments, were instituted of God, may be
questioned. Yet it is true that he holds men accountable for their acts in relation
to the governments which man has set up, and which are not approved of God.
(*Church History and Modern Revelation* [Salt Lake City: Deseret Book Company,
1953], 2:31.)

19. In view of the international scope of The Church of Jesus Christ of
Latter-day Saints, the following statement is applicable to Saints living under
different governmental systems: "A question has many times been asked of the
Church and of its individual members, to this effect: In the case of a conflict
between the requirements made by the revealed word of God, and those
imposed by the secular law, which of these authorities would the members of the
Church be bound to obey? In answer, the words of Christ may be applied—it is
the duty of the people to render unto Caesar the things that are Caesar's and unto
God the things that are God's. At present time the kingdom of heaven as an
earthly power, with a reigning King exercising direct and personal authority in
temporal matters, has not been established upon the earth. The branches of the
Church as such, and the members composing the same, are subjects of the several
governments within whose separate realms the Church organizations exist. In
this day of comparative enlightenment and freedom there is small cause for
expecting any direct interference with the rights of private worship and
individual devotion; in all civilized nations the people are accorded the right to
pray, and this right is assured by what may be properly called a common law of
humankind. No earnest soul is cut off from communion with his God; and with
such an open channel of communication, relief from burdensome laws and
redress for grievances may be sought from the power that holds control of
nations.

"Pending the overruling by Providence in favor of religious liberty, it is the duty of the saints to submit themselves to the laws of their country. Nevertheless, they should use every proper method, as citizens or subjects of their several governments, to secure for themselves and for all men the boon of freedom in religious service. It is not required of them to suffer without protect imposition by lawless persecutors, or through the operation of unjust laws; but their protests should be offered in legal and proper order. The saints have practically demonstrated their acceptance of the doctrine that it is better to suffer evil than to do wrong by purely human opposition to unjust authority. And if by thus submitting themselves to the laws of the land, in the event of such laws being unjust and subversive of human freedom, the people be prevented from doing the work appointed them of God, they are not to be held accountable for the failure to act under the higher law." (James E. Talmage, *Articles of Faith,* 29th edition [Salt Lake City, Utah: The Church of Jesus Christ of Latter-day Saints, 1960], pp. 422-23.)

20. Joseph Fielding Smith, *Church History and Modern Revelation* (Salt Lake City: Deseret Book Company, 1953), 1:462.

21. James R. Clark, ed., *Messages of the First Presidency,* 6 volumes (Salt Lake City: Bookcraft, 1966), 3:175.

22. McConkie, *A New Witness for the Articles of Faith,* (Salt Lake City: Deseret Book Company, 1985), p. 684.

23. *History of the Church* 3:295.

Epilogue

1. Gordon S. Wood, *The Creation of the American Republic, 1776-1787* (Chapel Hill: The University of North Carolina Press, 1969), p. 68. Wood is citing discourses from eighteenth-century writers.

2. Garry Wills, *Explaining America: The Federalist* (New York: Penguin Books, 1981), p. 270.

3. George Washington, letter to Marquis de Lafayette, *Writings of George Washington,* 1745-1799, edited by John C. Fitzpatrick (Washington, D.C.: U. S. Government Printing Office, 1939), 29:410.

4. George Washington, The First Inaugural Address, April 30, 1789, ibid., 30:294.

5. *Adams Family Correspondence,* 4 vols., L. H. Butterfield et al., eds. (Cambridge, Mass.: Harvard University Press, 1963), 2:21.

6. John Adams, *The Works of John Adams,* edited by C. F. Adams (Boston: Little, Brown Co., 1851), 4:31.

7. John R. Howe, Jr., *The Changing Political Thought of John Adams* (Princeton, New Jersey: Princeton University Press, 1966), p. 185.

8. *The Federalist Papers* (New York: The New American Library of World Literature, 1961), no. 57, p. 350.

9. Quoted in Jonathan Elliot, comp., *The Debates in the Several State Conventions on the Adoption of the Federal Constitution,* 5 vols. (Philadelphia: J.B. Lippincott Company, 1901), 2:536-37; italics added.

10. *The Federalist Papers,* no. 76, p. 458.

11. Wills, *Explaining America,* p. 269.

12. Ibid., pp. 268, 270.

13. Morton Borden, ed., *The Antifederalist Papers* (East Lansing: Michigan State University Press, 1965), p. 159.

14. *Notes of The Debates in the Federal Convention of 1787 Reported by James Madison* (Athens, Ohio: Ohio University Press, 1966), p. 654.

15. Ibid., p. 656.

16. Albert Henry Smyth, ed., *The Writings of Benjamin Franklin,* 10 volumes (New York: The Haskell House Publishers, 1970), 9:569.

17. "The State of American Values," *U. S. News and World Report,* December 9, 1985, pp. 52, 57.

18. Ibid., pp. 52, 55. The findings of the survey published by *U. S. News and World Report* was based on a survey conducted by the Roper Organization with more than a thousand Americans over the age of eighteen.

19. Ibid., p. 58.

20. Terry Eastland, "Teaching Morality in Public Schools," *Wall Street Journal,* February 22, 1982.

21. Ezra Taft Benson, "Cleansing the Inner Vessel," *Ensign,* May 1986, pp. 4-7.

Index